Coping WITH PETS

PETER COREY

Illustrated by Martin Brown

Scholastic Children's Books,
Scholastic Publications Ltd,
7–9 Pratt Street, London NW1 0AE, UK

Scholastic Inc.,
555 Broadway, New York, NY 10012-3999,
USA

Scholastic Canada Ltd,
123 Newkirk Road, Richmond Hill,
Ontario, Canada L4C 3G5

Ashton Scholastic Pty Ltd,
PO Box 579, Gosford, New South Wales,
Australia

Ashton Scholastic Ltd,
Private Bag 94407, Greenmount, Auckland,
New Zealand

First published by Scholastic Publications Ltd, 1995

Text copyright © Peter Corey, 1995
Illustrations copyright © Martin Brown, 1995

ISBN: 0 590 55838 2

Printed by Cox and Wyman Ltd, Reading, Berks
10 9 8 7 6 5 4 3 2 1

Contents .....

Foreword

A pet is not a toy. Oh, sorry – that's six words.

Dedication –

This book is dedicated to:
Sadie, Flash, Bumble, Bugsie, Splodge, Chockie, Blackie, Darkie, Bob, Solo, Chloe, Snuggles, Bertie Lookalike, Thomas Longjump, The Ironing Board Caterpillars, the mice (forget the names, can't forget the smell), thingy the tortoise (also gone, also forgotten), the ferret (not really a pet, more of a working animal), the rabbit (not really a pet, more of a lunch – thanks to the ferret) and all the other four/three/two-legged furred or feathered creatures who have struggled bravely and petfully to enrich my life – and failed miserably.

I would like to thank the following

Obviously a book like this can't just be thrown together, even though it might appear to have been! I had to do a bit of reading, question-asking and general brain-picking.[1] Because of this, I would like to thank the following people:

ANIMAL MAGIC, Margate, Kent.
DOOLITTLES PETSHOP, Cliftonville, Kent.

I would also like to suggest that – in addition to reading my book – you might like to dip into the following. I did, and found them very helpful:

New Observer's Book of Pets by Tina Hearne
Published by Penguin Books Limited
People and Pets by Bruce Fogel
Published by Boxtree Limited
Funfax – Unusual Pets by Chris Madsen
Published by Henderson Publishing
Pet Facts by Mike Geary BVSc., FRCVS
Published by HarperCollins
Presidential Pets by Niall Kelly
Published by Abbeville Press
Dogs and Puppies by Rose Hill
Published by Usborne Publishing Limited
How The Animals Do It by Larry Feign
English edition published by Souvenir Press Limited
Complete Guide To British Wildlife by R. and A. Fitter
Published by HarperCollins

1: I also had to get a lot closer to some animals than I frankly consider good for a person.

Pets — who's keeping who?

Since the dawning of time "Man" and "beast" have lived side by side in harmony. Or so the poets and suchlike would have us believe. But even only a basic knowledge of the world's history will tell you that this is rubbish. Poetic (probably) but rubbish all the same. The simple fact is that animals were here first. Whatever theory you believe in about the creation of the Earth, everybody accepts that dinosaurs were the first creatures on the planet.[1] And, despite anything you may have thought from watching *The Flintstones*, there were no humans on Earth at that time.[2] The Bible, for instance, clearly states that God made heaven, Earth, land, sea, grass, herbs, trees, stars, day, night, Sun, Moon, whales, birds, cows etc., and finally humans,[3] in that order.

HMM... WHAT CAN I DO WITH THESE SCRAGGY LEFT OVERS?

1: Well, the first things that were even half-way attractive in a Hollywood box office sort of way anyway!
2: I must admit I used to think there were. I stopped thinking this a few years after I realized that *The Flintstones* was a cartoon, and not real people.
3: Yes! We were considered less important than a sprig of parsley!

Even ancient civilizations who believed that the Earth is flat had to admit that animals came first, because they believed that the world was a disc, balancing on the back of four elephants, who in turn were balancing on the back of a great turtle.

So if animals were here before us, why do we keep *them* as pets, instead of the other way round? Well, the short answer is, we don't. No. The fact of the matter is that we don't keep pets, animals *allow themselves* to be kept by us. Now you may think that that is an outrageous (not to say silly) thing to say. But that is exactly what I shall be arguing throughout this book, and hopefully proving. So there!

But why do animals allow themselves to be kept as pets? Well, think about it. Imagine for a moment that you're an animal. Compare a life in the wild to life as a "pet": being prey to the elements (not to mention other animals), instead of curled up on a carpet watching *The Really Wild Show* and thinking "those penguins must be freezing. They should get themselves a nice little Barratt Home like mine. OK, so it's got some humans in it, but they're not here all the time, and at least they can work a tin-opener!" Compare having to hunt around for food instead of having it collected for you from a supermarket, paid for by somebody else. Imagine having a warm comfortable bed instead of having to fight over an old cardboard box with a bunch of other displaced animals (some of them human). I know which I'd go for. OK, so you'd have to let the humans pick you up occasionally and stroke you; you'd have to let them pretend they own you. But surely it's a small price to pay if they're picking up the tab for everything else.

When you get your pet you may, not unreasonably, feel that you have saved him/her from – at worst – a nasty cruel world and – at best – an overcrowded pet

shop with a very noisy smelly parrot that nobody, including the owners, can stand. The parrot of course knows this, and delights in biting every potential customer, thus shortening the other pets' hopes of escape. You may also feel that, having done this good deed, your pet should perhaps feel a small sense of gratitude. Animals do not see it that way at all. What you are entering into is – in their eyes at least – a full and equal partnership. If you don't believe me try this simple test: go up to your dog/cat – he's the one lying in the most comfortable chair in the room – and say: "Oi! Get out of that chair at once!" quite firmly but not nastily.

Now watch his reaction. Does he:

a) leap from the chair with a look that says: "Sorry! No, I'm really really sorry! I had absolutely no idea that was your chair! I thought it was my basket! I'm really that stupid! This isn't an act!"[1]

b) pretend not to hear, even when you repeat it through a loudhailer;

c) get out of the chair very slowly and deliberately, never losing eye contact, and then wander aimlessly around for a while, plonking himself down on the very spot of floor where you were just about to put your coffee cup?

If the reaction is c), this is exactly what I would expect. That look is saying: "OK, matey, just this once. But just wait till I get my can-opener GCSE in night-school, I'll be out of here and you won't see me for dust."

If the reaction is b), then this is just a subtler version of c).

If the reaction is a), then this is no pet. This is an actor in a skin.

Incidentally, when your hamster charges around the room in one of those plastic hamster balls, that look of grim determination on his face is caused by him thinking: "If I can just get up enough speed, I could probably bounce into that chair!" Because this is the thing about pets. Once they have allowed you to buy them and take them into your home, they regard the relationship not as that of pet and owner, but more like house sharing. Flatmates, if you like.

1: Actually in the case of most dogs, this is true. They really are that stupid. But they are also too stupid to realize that they really are that stupid. (*See* **Dog**)

The Pet Through History

But why is it that humans never realize this? Why do they always naturally assume that a pet will be over the moon[1] at being "owned"? It's hard to tell. The simple truth is that Man has always surrounded himself with animals. Perhaps it was through some strange misguided belief that it would in some way prove that he was the superior species. If that was the case then it hasn't worked. Any pet owner will tell you that they don't feel superior to their pet – often far from it! So why do we do it?

Well, in order to even attempt to answer that we should examine the role of the pet throughout history . . .

The civilization of dawn – or the lunch that got away

Humans have not always regarded animals as good pet material, despite claims to the contrary. No – the truth is that the prehistoric land was a bleak and barren place[2] with little or no vegetation. Man had to eat anything he could chuck a pointy stick at. As technology increased, with inventions such as the wheel, Man realized that animals could be useful. They could help out, while they were waiting to be eaten.

After all, standing around doing nothing would only make them fatty and high in cholesterol. By harnessing a horse, for instance, to the front of a cart, that same

1: Actually there has only ever been one reported sighting of a pet going over the moon, and as this was a domestic animal – a cow – and as the only witness was a dog who was laughing at the time, I think we can discount it, don't you?
2: A lot of it still is, or certainly soon will be.

horse[1] could help Man transport his animals to the slaughter house. Dogs too could be used to retrieve any birds that Man had shot. This was something dogs did naturally – the hard part was getting them to hand over the bird once they'd retrieved it.

Armoured and pyjama-ed

The Age of Chivalry, more than any other period in history, was particularly badly named. Not only did knights in armour go around killing each other, but they found new and more imaginative ways of using animals, as you will see from this beautifully reproduced brass rubbing.

As you can see, life was so unpredictable that knights had to be ready for battle at all times.[2] In order to achieve this they were forced to sleep in full armour, clutching their sword, so that at a moment's

---

1: Many countries had decided that the average horse looked a lot more appetizing with a jockey on its back rather than barbecue sauce on its ribs.
2: Day and knight in fact! Ho-ho!

notice they could summon the six men and the winch that it would take to get them to a standing position and go into battle. But what is the dog doing? Well, I don't know whether you've ever slept in a full suit of armour, but it's not warm. Mainly because it has little gaps and no fleecy lining. So, in order not to freeze to death on the eve of battle, knights of old devised an early form of hot water bottle. They filled a small dog up with boiling water, and as long as the dog was stupid enough to keep its mouth shut all night, it would remain warm.

Not that this was the only example of the imaginative use of an animal.

The empire: stiff upper lip and don't lose your head

The Victorians, of course, were masters at using animals for really no good purpose. They would travel to foreign countries, seek out exotic and beautiful animals, shoot them, and then hang the animal's head on their wall. The purpose of this was, I suppose, so that they could have conversations along the lines of:

> "Ah! I see you have an elephant's head on your wall."
> "Yes."

I suppose the explorers felt that they were doing the world a great service bringing these animals to their attention. Not that that justifies killing them, although maybe that was the only way they could get them on the boat:

Not that the Victorians killed all the wild animals they caught, oh no. Many they shipped back home and placed in zoos. Not as much fun as roaming free in vast areas of unpopulated country you might say, but at least it was more fun than having your head stuck over somebody's fireplace. I suppose. I don't know, never having had to face that choice.

The underdog bites back

So, given the terrible times that many animals have had to suffer at the hand of Man throughout the centuries, how do animals get their own back? Well, wild animals don't. Oh, yes, sure, they eat the odd person, but that's only a sort of tit-for-tat and doesn't really count. Domestic animals can't really do very much. Many are largely bred for food, and know no other life. It is left to the domestic pet to redress the balance. To right the wrongs done to their ancestors. And they do – with a vengeance!

THIS ONE'S FOR YOU, GREAT, GREAT, GREAT UNCLE BERT!

Coping with pets – dealing with humans

Revenge – as they say – is sweet. And in the case of pets, the revenge starts the minute you look through the window of the pet shop/visit the zoo/holiday on the farm, etc. You see, all animals on display have one thing in common: they are *cute*. Yes! They are. Even the Vietnamese pot-bellied pig is attractive to somebody, believe it or not.

In the case of animals that are traditionally pet-material,[1] it is a very small step from: "Isn't it cute?" to: "Can we buy it?"

And that, dear reader, is where the trouble starts. Consider this very common scenario:

1: As opposed to pet food.

At the pet shop

This is the situation: you are walking down the road, minding your own business, when suddenly you become aware of a pair of sad little eyes boring into the back of your neck. What do you do? You make your first mistake, that's what you do. Instead of doing what the owner of the sad little eyes would do if the roles were reversed, you stop. And look. And get hooked.

Mistake number two coming up: your parent is probably with you. They are supposed, traditionally, to save you from danger. Protect you from the unknown. Help you when you're out of your depth.[1] And to be fair they do say: "Come on! You're going to be late for the dentist!" Which of course would never do! Dentists get withdrawal if they are kept waiting more than a few minutes when they could be inflicting pain. And it almost works. You almost turn away from the window. And then you hear a voice: "It couldn't do any harm to look, could it?" Was it you? Was it your parent? Was it some fragment of a total stranger's conversation drifting into your ear quite by chance? Who knows? Either way you are about to make mistake number three:

You are inside the pet shop. Even the smell is comforting. It doesn't smell of animals that people have forgotten to clean out for months. It smells of open sacks of grain and warm fur. It smells of cosy things. Even that noisy parrot sounds quite musical, and – certainly during all the time you are in the shop – he inflicts no fatal wounds on unsuspecting customers. And it is inside the shop that the "ah!" factor suddenly kicks in. The cute little kittens in the window are just the tip of the iceberg. There are lop-eared rabbits,[2] lovebirds,

1: That's the theory anyway!
2: Who always look to me as though they've been involved in some terrible experiment to prove that you really shouldn't pick rabbits up by their ears.

budgerigars, canaries, fish, gerbils, hamsters, white mice and, of course, puppies! Lots of puppies! Little bundles of fluff falling over each other to get to the wire and be touched by the human hand of kindness. How can we resist? We can't. Already we are discussing the relative cost of gerbils with the petshop boys. Mistake number four!

This is amazing! How have we got from "Well, we'll just have a look" to "I cannot live without that puppy"[1] in a matter of seconds? It isn't even as though there has been any hard sell on the part of the owners. If fact most pet shop people are very laid-back, half asleep, almost. They do say that being surrounded by animals can have this effect on you, unless of course it's a pack of wolves. So there you are, emerging from the pet shop to go and book a pantechnicon to transport the accessories – you know the type of thing: special cage/box/basket, special brush, special bowl, special vitamins, special economy-sized sack of Multi-mixer All-Purpose Pet Food.[2]

Why do pet shops always try to sell you these massive sacks of food? I'll tell you: it's their subtle way of saying: "He's yours now. We don't want him back at any price!" Because they already know what you have yet to discover: pets are trouble! You don't believe me? Read on!

1: Or guppy, if you're a fish person.
2: What on Earth is All-Purpose Pet Food? What purpose does it serve other than to be eaten by pets, I'd like to know?

Pets - from small puddle to raging storm

Animals know instinctively that they are basically unattractive. They are largely anti-social, they have unpleasant habits, and – probably worst of all – they don't care. That's the way they like to be. It's the way they're meant to be. It's the way a lot of us would love to be, given half a chance, but we know that we wouldn't get away with it. But animals can – and do. Just answer me this:

What is the first thing a puppy does the minute you get it home? Yes – it wees all over you. What is the one thing it didn't do in the shop, or on the homeward journey? That's right – wee all over anybody. And believe me there were probably a few people on that bus who deserved it! But the little . . . er . . . darling didn't do it until you arrived home because it was making a point. It was saying: "This is my house too and I'll do as I please". It didn't do it in the shop because you might have asked for your money back, or worse still not bought it at all. It didn't do it on the bus because there's probably a bylaw covering just that sort of offence. No. It did it in its own home. And the same is true of any pet you buy, although with mice it's probably less obvious. Now, an animal psychologist would probably tell you that it was only "marking its territory". This is *psychospeak*. It means "ruining the carpet".

But what can I do about it?

I hear that sad little plea. Well, the only thing you can do is learn to cope. If you understand what demands a particular pet is likely to make on you, you will be better equipped to deal with it. But be careful. You must have heard of animal cunning? Well, nobody has more of it than animals do. Which is probably why it's called *animal* cunning. Or, as I prefer to refer to it . . .

!!!!! Pet Power !!!!!

But what is Pet Power? Well, it's that little piece of knowledge that pets have (or believe they have) that makes them feel ultimately superior to humans. It might be the fact that they bite, when they look as though they wouldn't dream of it. It might be that they stink, when they look amazingly clean and well-groomed. It's a little something that pets believe gives them the upper hand, even though in many cases it doesn't because you are about a hundred times larger than they are for a start. But the fact that the pet believes it, is what makes that particular animal unstable. I have referred to this in the A–Z selection of this book as The Hidden Threat.

And if you can cope with this you are well on the way to coping with the animal in question. And that is what this book is all about . . .

Coping with pets

Throughout the rest of the book I will endeavour to tell you as much as I think you need to know about a particular type of pet. Enough certainly to keep you one step ahead and allow you to enjoy (as far as is possible) pet ownership. But never forget: a pet considers itself to be an unpaying guest in your house, and as such will expect to be extended at least as much courtesy as everyone else, if not more. So read on and take note . . .

Coping with this A-Z:

It couldn't be simpler. Well, it probably could be, but I don't know how, so it's like it is – OK?
Each entry is divided into the following categories:

What is it?

Straight away, this might strike you as a bit odd. You might be saying to yourself: "If I didn't know what it was I wouldn't be buying it, would I?" Well, all I can say to that is: "Don't you believe it!" You see, that's the thing about pets. You could go along to Petz-R-Uz to get a gerbil and come away with something that has a totally unpronounceable name that even David Attenborough wouldn't have the courage to poke with a pointy stick. Forewarned is forearmed (or four-legged).

What will it cost ?

This section will give you a rough guide to how much animals might cost you, or how – as in the case of insects[1] – you can collect them from the "wild". Of course this section only really  deals with the financial cost, not the cost to your health, sanity, etc.

Where will I keep it ?

Having got your pet home, you'll probably want to provide some kind of living quarters for it – unless of course it's a dog or a cat, in which case it'll probably take over your room while you doss down in the airing cupboard.

What will it eat ?

This is something that can be of vital importance when choosing a new pet. It's also useful if you're a first-time buyer, assuming of course that you don't fall into the trap of just going for "cute". So, before you take on this furry friend,[2] try saying something to the assistant along the lines of: "What about eating?" If they reply: "Try it roasted with mint sauce", you're probably in the butcher's, although this doesn't necessarily follow. If you're someone who isn't that good at looking after things, then the chances are that you are not going to be too

1: Actually it's not a good idea to keep insects in a case, unless they're going on their holidays.
2: It might not be furry. It might be a snake or a lizard. Incidentally, if it is a snake and furry, don't buy it. It'll probably turn out to be a giant caterpillar. This might be fun while it's still crawling around, but wait until it turns into a giant moth!

good at caring for anything that needs to be fed on some rare grass that can only be found on the sides of hillocks deep inside rain forests. So go for an animal that the pet shop person says will eat anything that comes in a tin with the words Pet Food on the side. Avoid anything that the pet shop person tells you eats furniture or people.[1]

1: You might feel tempted to go for something that they tell you eats younger brothers, but check first that the animal can tell the difference. You're unlikely to get a refund if you take it back and complain: "Here – you told me this thing ate younger brothers! Well, it ate me instead!"

What will it do ?

This section will cover everything from whether the pet will just sit there looking cute, or whether you will have to have everything valuable in the house wired to an electric current.[1] It will also cover whether or not your pet can be taught simple "tricks", although this is best avoided – partly because animals being made to perform can feel degraded, and partly because, if they get really good at it, they might insist on being paid!

Why do I want it ?

The reasons people get pets are many and various, but it is important that you ask yourself just why you want the pet before you commit yourself to it. Because they are a commitment. They do say that: "A pet is for life,

not just for Christmas." This is not strictly true, since most pets have a comparatively short life-span,[2] but your reasons for wanting a pet are still something that you should think about very carefully. Of course, no one could really blame you if you went into the pet shop with every intention of getting something sensible like a dog,[3] but came out with something unmanageable like a herd of wildebeest, for such is the Power of Pets, I'm afraid! Which brings us to . . .

1: A bit like when your baby brother was born!
2: Except in the case of the giant turtles from the Galápagos Islands.
3: *Sensible like a dog* is a contradiction in terms, of course.

When will it die?

This may seem a bit of a strange – not to say morbid – thing to ask a pet shop person, but it is certainly something you should consider. So, tactfully checking the average life expectancy of your chosen pet would be a good idea. Equally, tactfully checking that the animal is fit and healthy is also a good idea. After all, you don't want to spend your hard-earned pocket money on something that is going to keel over and die the minute it's exposed to direct sunlight.

A quick way of telling whether or not your pet is healthy enough to enjoy a long and happy life is to look at it in its surroundings. If its cage is surrounded by a medical "crash" team with billions of pounds' worth of life-saving equipment[1] and worried expressions, then the answer is probably no – it isn't going to last until you get it to the bus stop. If, however, you discover that your prospective pet has recently taken out a loan which involved it having a full medical, then the answer is probably yes – it is very, very healthy[2] and will probably live for ever.

Will it earn its keep ?

Mostly people get pets purely as pets – just animals to have around the place for no other reason than they fancy them being there. However, it's not impossible to want a "working" animal that is also a pet. If you live on a farm, for instance, you may want a pet horse which will also be involved in minor farm work.[3] If you live in

---

1: If it IS surrounded by all this gear, chances are this means that it can afford to "go private", so it's probably worth buying anyway as you might inherit.
2: If it HAS taken out a loan, don't buy it. Chances are it'll fall behind with the repayments, and you'll be left footing the bill.
3: Not milking the cows. Horses are notoriously bad at that.

a block of flats and only want something quite tiny – like a mouse – it's unlikely that you'll get him to do anything.[1] But naturally it is something to think about, particularly if the chosen animal is expensive to keep.

What will I call it ?

Giving your pet a name is a good idea. Most animals quickly learn to respond to having their name called, especially if the experience involves being given a meal at the end of it. But obviously you need to choose the right name for the type of animal. This section will help you do just that.

What else do I need to know ?

This section will deal with anything that I think you might need to know about a specific type of pet. It'll also include stuff about how to tell if your pet is a boy or a girl, and those sorts of things!

The hidden threat

This outlines the devious way in which a particular pet is working with its fellow animals to mess up your life.

So – those are the categories.

This is the A–Z OF PETS . . .

1: Although I did hear of a gerbil who had a paper round. He didn't hang on to it for long, though, because of his colour-blindness, which is not unusual in gerbils apparently. He kept muddling up the *TV* and *Radio Times*. He cost the newsagent hundreds of pounds in lost orders, not to mention thousands when the gerbil sued him for wrongful dismissal.

The A-Z of Pets

Ant

What is it?

Or perhaps we should really be asking: "*Where* is it?" As you know ants are very very small,[1] and because of this they aren't everybody's idea of a pet. But they do have a lot to offer for the keen enthusiast.[2] Experts point out that ants are extremely intelligent. So intelligent in fact that they could easily take over the world. Or at least they could if people didn't keep accidentally stepping on them. But because of this intelligence they do make fascinating pets. The other great "plus" of course is that you never have to groom or walk them!

OI! NOT SO FAST!

1: If you didn't know that then you do now, which must make you very pleased that you bought this book.
2: As they say in train-spotter magazines – not that I know from personal experience, you understand!

What will it cost ?

Well, in the case of ants, very little really, because you can pick them up *in the wild*. I've explained how you do this in the next section of the book. You can have a quick look now if you like – I don't mind waiting. Done it? Right. But you will need a queen ant. (*See last section of this entry.*)

Where will I keep it ?

Ants live in an ant colony. And this is what your queen will create. No fancy palace for this girl, she'll be more than happy living in the ant nest that you've built for her out of dirt. I have explained in the next section of this wonderful book how to build suitable "homes" for your pet(s), and there's plenty of information on how to create a terrarium which will be suitable for an ant's nest. You can go and check now if you like, but I shan't wait for you this time, I'm afraid. I'm going to plough straight on. Sorry about that!

HMMM, ON THE OTHER HAND...

What will it eat?

At first, nothing. Queen Ant will be too busy laying her eggs. As the eggs hatch and the ants grow, they will start working to make the nest bigger. Now although, as I say, ants are very intelligent, it never occurs to them to take sandwiches to eat while they're working, so you'll have to provide food for them. Being related to bees they are very partial to a bit of bread and honey. They're not vegetarians, so the odd bit of minced beef will go down a treat. It's really a question of trial and error. Try them out with different things and see what they turn their noses up at.[1] Don't make the mistake of giving them a little menu so that they can order lunch, because although they are very bright they can't read.

What will it do?

Ants are fascinating. If you've built your terrarium properly you'll be able to watch them. Once the new babies hatch they soon grow up and become incredibly organized. The females either become workers who work, hunters who hunt, cleaners who clean or nannies who look after the next lot of babies. The male ants fly off and look for another young princess at another party.

1: You'll need a very strong magnifying glass to see this.

Why do I want it ?

Although an ant colony is quite tricky to set up, once your queen is in residence the rest takes care of itself. All you have to do is watch. But obviously the actual setting up is a lot of effort, if you're actually looking for something that you can take for walks or teach to juggle.

When will it die ?

Since it's pretty difficult to tell one ant from another, then it won't really matter if they die because you won't get that attached to individual ones. Also new queens will be born to replace the old one and the whole life-cycle will continue. The real question is how soon you will get bored.

Will it earn its keep ?

No is the short answer. No is the long answer as well, but since the cost of an ant colony is very little that won't really matter.

What will I call it ?

Of course you can go through the pantomime of giving all your ants names,[1] but short of providing them all with minute dog tags it will be more or less impossible to keep track of them. Also, it's unlikely that they will stop to acknowledge you if you call their names. They work to a very tight schedule and haven't got time for idle gossip.

1: Naming them after the last England football squad to win the World Cup is a good idea, if you can find anybody who can remember their names.

What else do I need to know?

Catching your queen isn't the tricky part – finding her is. However, once a year the ants throw a huge party. It's a kind of "coming-out" for the new young queens (I suppose at this point they are princesses). Anyway, all the lads turn up for the party. Well, as with most parties where there are no "grown-ups", one thing leads to another, the young princess becomes a queen, her wings drop off and she starts looking for somewhere to set up home and lay her eggs.

And it is at this point, and only at this point, that you can catch your queen. Maybe you could put up a very tiny notice saying "Palace to let – suit young queen about to have large family", although this'll probably be a complete waste of time because ants, as I've already mentioned, can't read – which is surprising really because they are, as I've said, amazingly intelligent.

The hidden threat

On the face of it ants aren't really a threat. After all, if they start getting a bit uppity you can tread on them. That might seem a bit extreme, but still. No, the way in which ants are going to mess up your life, and they'll do this anyway whether you decide to keep them as pets or not, is to come on picnics with you. You have been warned!

Bee

Bees are worth a mention, although keeping them is a specialized art. If you are ever interested in keeping bees, then chat to a proper bee-keeper, and I'm sure they'll give you better advice than I can. But here are a few pointers: bees belong to the same family as ants, although they are the richer branch of the family because they can afford those nice fluffy stripey jumpers. But a colony of bees works in much the same way as an ant colony, with workers, nannies, etc. The major difference is that bees make honey, so they can easily earn their own keep, unlike ants who just make very tiny holes in the ground.

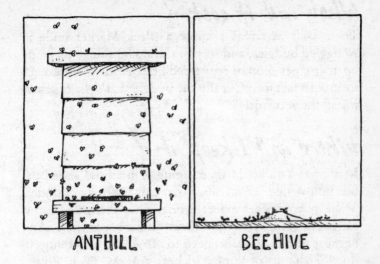

ANTHILL   BEEHIVE

Bird

See **Budgerigar/Chicken/Parrot**

Budgerigar

What is it?

A small brightly coloured bird. They were first imported
to this country from Australia in around 1840, so they
stopped wearing corks round their hats years ago.
Nowadays they are just as likely to be found in East-
bourne, where they have gained quite a reputation as
being perfect companions for old people. Not that
budgies – as they are affectionately known – just go for
old people. Oh, no! They'll peck anybody.

What will it cost ?

There isn't as far as I know a Black Market trade in smuggled budgies, and so you should be able to pick one up at any pet shop or registered breeder for as little as £5 to £10. In fact it isn't really the budgie that's the expense, it's all the accessories.

Where will I keep it ?

In a cage. You could try keeping it in an old shoe box, but you would soon realize that this is not a good idea. Make sure you get a decent one, since the little chap is probably going to spend the rest of his life in there. And because of this, you also need to provide it with things to do. "What sort of things?" I hear you say. Well, I'll tell you if you give me a chance!

Budgies are very pretty, and boy, don't they know it. One of the things they really like is looking at themselves in the mirror. So the first essential accessory for the cage is a mirror. Next you'll need a perch. It is quite likely that the cage already has some, but make sure that you've got one that can be positioned so that the budgie can sit on it and look at himself in the mirror. Next a swing, cunningly arranged so that no matter how high the budgie swings he can still see himself in the mirror. Next a ladder, running to and from the mirror and any other "viewing points". Next a bell. Some mirrors already have these, but if not you'll need to get one. The purpose of this bell may not be obvious straight away, but after observing your budgie for even a short time you'll realize that they do nod off quite a bit. The bell is there so that they can wake themselves up. After all, they don't want to waste valuable mirror-gazing time, do they?

What will it eat?

Well, of course it's quite likely that, after filling the cage with accessories, there's no room left for food dispensers. There may not even be any room for the bird, which would solve the feeding problem at a stroke. But, assuming you have got a decent-sized cage, and not turned it into a multi-gym, you will need a small shallow bowl and a water dispenser. You should attach the water dispenser to the side of the cage, making sure that the bird can watch himself drinking without either dribbling on his beautiful plumage or breaking his neck. His food bowl should contain mixed seed. Check with the pet shop as to which type to buy, but the really important thing is that the bowl should not be too far away from the mirror. This is because budgies can't go too long without looking at themselves, and you don't want it to starve.

What will it do?

I would have thought that was obvious – look at itself in the mirror. It is also possible to teach Budgie to talk, although whatever you try to teach them, they always wind up saying: "Who's a pretty boy, then?"

Why do I want it?

Good question, although as I have said, they are entertaining, and it's always handy to have a budgie around – if only to serve as a constant reminder that there is at least one other creature on the planet who spends more time staring at themselves in the mirror than your older brother/sister!

When will it die?

The average budgie will live for about five to six years, although they can live longer. They can also live a lot shorter, especially if you've got a cat! The main causes of death are:

a) incorrect diet – usually caused by letting it share the dog's dinner
b) skin tumours – usually caused by incorrect diet
c) heart attacks – usually caused by looking in the mirror and noticing a skin tumour.

Will it earn its keep ?

Well, not really. Although it might win the odd beauty contest, and repay you in that way.

What will I call it ?

You can call a budgie pretty well anything, although it'll probably end up calling itself "Joey". Because these birds are small and neat avoid names like "Hulk" and "Crusher".

What else do I need to know ?

Budgies do enjoy flying around, and if possible you should let it fly around the room. You could do this when you're cleaning out its cage, which you should do at least once a week. A word of warning though: make sure that all the windows are closed. Also make sure that there are no mirrors in the room, or you'll never get it back in the cage!

The hidden threat

On the face of it, budgies are no threat to you at all. They are pretty, personable and too small to be seriously dangerous. However, this is exactly how Pet Power works. Budgies have a great talent for letting out a really ear-piercing and totally pointless screech at the precise moment that you are trying to do something monumentally important: put the final touch to a particularly tricky school project, finish the final level of *The Lost Vikings* or some other computer sensation, hear the name of the mystery stranger who has decimated *Summer Bay* with a machine gun,[1] or even just thread a

1: So that you can write and thank him.

needle without skewering your thumb. Somehow that bird knows when to squawk to maximum devastating effect, without you suspecting for one minute that he did it on purpose.

Bush cricket

What is it?

A cricket is a large insect related to the grasshopper.

What will it cost?

Well, nothing, as long as you can catch one. But before you start getting all excited and saying: "Wow! My very own pet for nothing! Gimme gimme!" you should only keep them for a few days because they really don't like living in captivity – and that is the way your average cricket would view living in your house. You may well have come to the same conclusion. To catch your cricket you have to go out on a warm night and listen. If you can hear nothing but the roar of passing traffic, you might be standing in the middle of a motorway, which is really not a good place to find crickets – not live ones, anyway.[1] If you can hear the song of the cricket,[2] then you'll know that male crickets are nearby. Only the males sing. The females are bright enough to keep quiet just in case there's some dork with a jam-jar hanging around waiting to capture them.

1: The middle of a motorway is no place for any living thing to be found wandering around.
2: Music and lyrics by Sir Andrew Lloyd Webber, probably. After all, he's written everything else.

Where will I keep it?

Not in a jam-jar, that's for sure. And this is really what makes keeping this particular pet a bit of a pain, because you'll need to set up a terrarium (*see* **A Home of Their Own**), so you'll need to be pretty sure of being able to find other crickets as replacements once you've let one lot go. And the big problem here is how to tell which ones have already stayed at your house and which ones haven't, because they're not likely to let you know by coming up to you and saying: "Blimey! Doesn't your dad shout a lot!"

What will it eat?

Bush crickets eat fruit, soft plants and other vegetables. Some of them, anyway. Others will only eat meat. The best thing to do is give them what you think they'll like, and if they turn their noses up at it, kick them out. Otherwise you are going to run yourself ragged trying to please them, and in no time at all you'll hear yourself saying things to them like: "You treat this place like a hotel!" Which of course is exactly what it is to them, except that they didn't book it through Thomas Cook – they were hijacked. Actually, I suppose it's a bit more like a time-share than a hotel in that way!

What will it do?

Stand around banging its legs together. Sing. Er . . . that's it. They aren't really staying long enough to do much else. If you put plenty of twigs and so on in the terrarium, they might climb up them. Then again they might not.

Why do I want it?

Again this is a very good question, and one that you should definitely ask yourself. Because although they are interesting, it is quite a lot of effort for a couple of days.[1]

When will it die?

If you keep a bush cricket in captivity more than a couple of days, it will almost certainly die.

Will it earn its keep?

Not at all. It's a non-paying guest, remember.

What will I call it?

You won't know it long enough to need to give it a name. You can if you want to, but don't get upset if, once it's moved on, you don't get a card saying: "Hi! This is Roger! I really enjoyed staying with you!" Bush crickets just aren't like that.

1: This attitude is not uncommon in humans too. I've stayed in a number of hotels where the staff seem to think that it's not worth making an effort for somebody who's only staying a couple of days.

What else do I need to know?

If you want to tell the difference between male and female crickets – if, for instance, your little terrarium Hotel (you could call it Bide-a-Wee) has strict rules about unmarried crickets sharing living quarters – then it might be useful for you to know that the male cricket has two little spikes on his bottom. This makes it very difficult for him to sit down, I imagine, and probably explains why he's always on the move. Females, on the other hand, have a long horn thing sticking out of their bottoms. They use this to drill a hole in the ground in which to bury their eggs. This is just one of the wonderful ways that Mother Nature helps those poor creatures that have neither the body strength nor the technical know-how to work a Black and Decker drill.

The hidden threat

The ways of Pet Power are many and devious. And the cricket is more subtle than most. Caring for "dumb creatures" is a built-in human instinct, and the cricket knows this. We do it often in the vain hope that we might be shown some affection back. Forget it! Crickets will come and stay, eat your bread, climb up your stick, and leave without a word of thanks. And you'll probably never hear from them again – not even a postcard. Sad, really.

See also **House Cricket**

Canary

(*See also* **Budgerigar**)

The main difference between budgies and canaries is that canaries are yellow and budgies can be. Canaries also used to work down coal mines. Now nobody does. They were used to check for gas leaks, so presumably – unlike budgies – canaries can be taught to say: "I smell gas."

Because of this additional talent, a canary is about £5 more expensive than a budgie.

NAY NAY LAD...THERE'S NOWT FOR THEE DOWNT' PIT, THA WANTST' GET INT' PET TRADE

The hidden threat

Well, the possibility that, unless you're really nice to it, it might forget to say: "I smell gas."

Cat

What is it?

The ancient Egyptians used to worship cats. They were obviously not stupid, even if their empire didn't stand the test of time. They started keeping cats to catch mice. The rest of the world were using weasels and ferrets at the time. Although the Egyptians tried to protect and hide their cats, some inevitably escaped and spread over the rest of the world. Thus the domestic cat came into being. Isn't that fascinating? Well, I thought it was, anyway!

Cats have always been lumped together with dogs as ideal domestic pets, but they really couldn't be more different. Dogs are pack animals, and are therefore very sociable. Cats hunt alone, and are very much their own animal. If you intend to keep a cat, expect only to see it when it feels like dropping in – usually at meal times. Also expect only to touch it when it wants you to – usually never. The average cat is anything up to about half a metre long. If your cat is two metres long and eats the neighbours, it's probably a tiger.

MOGGY

TIGER

What will it cost ?

It's hard to say exactly what a cat would cost to buy. It could be free – if you get it from the lady up the road. It could, however, cost £20, £30, or £40 (or more) depending on its breed and pedigree.

Where will I keep it ?

Cats like to come and go as they please. A cat flap is a good idea, allowing a cat to get into the house when it pleases. However, if your family does fit a cat flap, make sure that your moggy doesn't start bringing home dozens of his mates for a late-night rave-up.[1] Cats can sleep out of doors, as long as they've got a warm bed – a bit like humans, really!

What will it eat ?

Cats are carnivorous. That means they eat meat. Now, cats aren't fussy. You can either provide it for them out of a tin, or they'll go out for a takeaway bird or mouse. But if you're thinking, "Oh good! That'll save a bit of cash!" think again. Because not only will Moggy bring himself a takeaway birdie, he'll probably bring you one as well!

1: Also check, before you lobby for a cat flap, that there are no really, really small burglars operating in your area.

What will it do?

It's hard to say. Based on what you see him do, then the answer will probably be "sleep". But based on what he's actually doing, well – if you can imagine it, Moggy's probably doing it!

Why do I want it?

Cats, probably more than any other animal, are really interesting because they are as like humans as animals ever really get – although I think most cats would be insulted by that remark. They do what they want to do, and if you don't like it – tough! Perhaps you don't want an animal that is a constant reminder of just how many things parents and other grown-ups don't let you get away with. So, if you don't want to feel depressed, don't have a cat.

When will it die?

It depends. Cats are quite fond of climbing inside car engines and going into that kind of deep sleep – catatonic, I think it's called – that prevents them hearing the car starting up. But if you keep them properly, and make sure they get their injections, boosters, meals, etc., they can live for about 12 to 15 years. Some even longer. Whether they'll actually stay living *with you* is another matter!

Will it earn its keep?

No. And if you try to teach it tricks or anything like that, it'll let you know exactly what it thinks of you!

What will I call it?

As an actor, I know several people who have cats named after characters from Shakespeare plays – Titania, Macbeth, Titus Andronicus. Not a good idea. But then, whatever you call your cat, it will probably take no notice, so call it anything you like. But be careful, because the time may come that you feel compelled to stand on the doorstep and yell (pointlessly) for your cat to come home. It's then that you'll wish you'd called it something other than Fat Bottom.

What else do I need to know?

Nothing really. Owning a cat immediately puts you on a learning curve,[1] and your cat will waste no time in letting you know if you're getting it wrong.

1: In the case of cats this is more of a learning helter-skelter.

The hidden threat

On the face of it you might think that you know exactly where you are with a cat. However most cat owners are taken in by the images of cats on greetings cards, not to mention the vulnerability that kittens project.[1] This is entirely false, but such is Pet Power that we poor humans still persevere in treating cats as we treat dogs, and expecting them to respond in kind. Forget it! It is not going to happen!

Caterpillar

What is it ?

A caterpillar is the lava (or baby) of a moth or butterfly.

What will it cost ?

Nothing. In the spring or autumn you can find them almost anywhere. Well, not exactly anywhere. I mean you're not going to find them in your pyjama pocket, unless you live in a bush.

Where will I keep it ?

In a terrarium (*see* **A Home of Their Own**). You'll need earth in the bottom of your terrarium, so that eventually the caterpillar can hide in order for it to pupate.

1: A vulnerability, incidentally, that disappears the minute you get it home!

What will it eat?

Contrary to popular belief, caterpillars are quite fussy eaters. But, since caterpillars tend to stand on leaves while they are eating,[1] the best thing to do is get plenty of whatever he was standing on when you caught him, and put that in with him. But be careful: if he was standing on a house-brick when you spotted him, chances are he wasn't trying to eat it, he was just en route to the next alfresco café.[2] In which case try placing him on a few different leaves and see which takes his fancy.

What will it do?

Initially a caterpillar will eat leaves. If you put some twigs in with him he'll climb them, but only if there's a leaf at the end of them. The reason he's doing this is to fatten himself (or herself, obviously!) up ready for when it's time to pupate. When the time arrives, he'll probably dig himself into the ground or hang on to a twig, and a hard shell will build up around him, called a *chrysalis*. He'll stay like this for some months. As you might imagine, this is when your pet is at his least interesting.

1: Cor! Imagine the trouble you'd get into if you started walking all over your food!
2: Likewise if he's standing on a leaf with another caterpillar, it could be that he doesn't like it at all, but he's on a heavy date so doesn't want to appear rude by throwing up. Nature is complicated!

When he eventually emerges – and if it's a cold winter he might wait until it's over before he does this – he will be either a moth or a butterfly. This is when he is at his most interesting. And – surprise, surprise! – this is when you have to let him go!

BORING CATERPILLAR

LESS BORING CHRYSALIS

INTERESTING BUTTERFLY

Why do I want it?

I don't know. I must admit that I have kept caterpillars, but ultimately they are very disappointing.

When will it die?

It won't as long as you feed it. Well, it will eventually, but it will have left your care by then, so you won't actually be around to see it.

Will it earn its keep?

No.

What will I call it?

Caterpillar would seem to be a good name. Or Horace. Or Doris. Or anything really.

What else do I need to know?

Nothing. I think I've told you everything. I may even have dressed it up slightly to make it more riveting than it actually is.

The hidden threat

The caterpillar is another example of a temporary pet that is ultimately totally unrewarding. The added feature of this creature is that it seems to know instinctively the exact moment when you start getting interested in it, because within minutes it turns into a chrysalis. And what is more it does it on purpose!

Chicken

What is it?

A chicken is a fowl. It is also foul, which you'll know if you've got any sense of smell at all. It is also incredibly ugly. Now, chickens know that they are ugly. Consequently they know that you haven't taken them into your home because you're stunned by their beauty, oh no. They know exactly why they are there: eggs, and possibly lunch. So – if you decide to keep chickens, be prepared for a fair amount of sulking.

What will it cost?

Really you should keep more than one chicken. This increases the potential morning egg delivery, and lessens the birds' paranoia about being eaten. Chickens cost around £8 each, but that is just the tip of the iceberg.

Where will I keep it?

You will need a chicken run, and a chicken house. This takes up quite a bit of room, so chickens are not ideal if you live in a flat. You would be well advised to get the run before getting any chickens, mainly because there is no way that the lazy little devils will offer to help you build it.

What will it eat?

Chicken feed, although it will certainly cost more than that, because – like most pets – chickens have developed expensive tastes. At one time a chicken would eat old spud peel and so on, but not now. Oh, no – now they want a proper balanced feed. However, it's worth it, because the better the quality of the food, the better the taste of the eggs (and so forth!).

51

What will it do?

Well, not a lot, to be honest. I've always thought that "chicken run" was a silly name for the thing you keep chickens in, because they don't really do a lot of running. It should really be called something like the "chicken peck" or the "chicken squawk" or the "chicken stand-around-looking-unbelievably-stupid". But they do lay eggs, which will probably turn out to be the only good reason for keeping them. As long as you like eggs.

Why do I want it?

As I've said earlier, chickens aren't everybody's idea of the perfect pet, so if you are thinking of getting some you're probably thinking of keeping them in order to make money. If this is the case you might be better using the money to buy British Telecom shares. After all, have you seen how much your big brother and sister use the phone? You'll be a millionaire overnight.

When will it die?

When your mum suddenly remembers that your Auntie Freda is coming to Sunday dinner and the shops are shut.

Will it earn its keep?

Yes. If only by selling the eggs. Obviously the more chickens you have the more eggs you'll get, but then you would also need more room, it would cost more for feed, etc., so if you are keeping them in order to become a multi-national egg company, or even just to make a bit of pocket money – be careful. Make sure you've done your sums correctly in the first place.

What will I call it?

Henny-Penny, Chicken-Lickin, Kentucky Fried – whatever you choose you can be fairly sure that it'll have great trouble living up to it.

What else do I need to know?

It's a strange fact, but if you cut a chicken's head off it'll carry on running around for a good ten minutes. This makes it the only animal on the planet that can actually watch itself doing the birdie dance.

If you want to know the difference between a male chicken (cockerel) and a female (hen), then it's this: a hen lays eggs, a cockerel wakes you up very, very early in the morning.

The hidden threat

Well – in the case of the male, or cockerel, you might come to rely on it as an alarm clock.[1] Don't. The one day you need to get up early, old "Cocky" will decide to have a lie-in! The hidden threat from the female, or hen, is will she or won't she lay? I know some people who keep chickens who are totally obsessed with this. Pet Power at its most sneaky.

1: Or alarm cock.

Chipmunk

What is it?

If you've ever watched the *Chipmunks* cartoon on TV, you might think that a chipmunk is a cute little thing that sings in a speeded-up voice. It isn't. It's a fast-moving squirrelly sort of thing that bites. There are 21 different varieties, and some bite more than others.

fig 1.

BITUS HORRIBILUS   BITUS NASTIUS   BITUS MAXIMUS

BITUS AWFULUS   BITUS EVILUS   BITUS TERRIBLUS

What will it cost?

A chipmunk can cost around £25, depending on where you buy it.[1] But the big expense is the cage. Chipmunks need a lot of room, because they do like rushing about. A pair of chipmunks would need a cage at least a metre square and maybe two metres high, with plenty of branches and suchlike for them to jump from. This is something that it would probably be as well to make. So work out the cost in advance.

Where will I keep it?

Oh, sorry, I've just told you that!

1: None of the major supermarkets ever have them on special offer.

What will it eat?

Chipmunks will eat nuts and seeds, but they also like fruit and berries. They are also not above eating insects, birds' eggs and small brothers – sorry! I mean small rodents. OK, so they're same thing. Like hamsters they have food pouches in their cheeks, so they can carry great mouthfuls of food around with them. This may lead you to think that they won't bite with their mouth full.[1] Don't you believe it!

What will it do?

Chipmunks are very, very active. This makes them interesting to watch. But watch is really all you can do, unless you're wearing a complete suit of armour.

LOOK THERE HE IS, NO THERE, NO OVER THERE, NO THERE... THERE THAT'S HIM, NO THERE!

1: After all, your mum is always telling your little brother that it's rude, isn't she?

When will it die ?

On average a male chipmunk will live for five years, a female for eight. I don't know why this should be, but since the male is the more aggressive of the two, it could be that eating too many human fingers is really bad for them!

Will it earn its keep ?

Well, no. Unless of course I'm wrong about them being able to sing in a speeded-up voice, in which case they'll probably land a recording contract and their own TV series. If this happens they will almost certainly deny ever knowing you, so be warned!

MY EX-OWNER, WHAT A PLEB

What will I call it ?

Well, Alvin if you want to be really obvious. Nipper or Biter if you want to be really honest.

What else do I need to know ?

Chipmunks breed twice a year, in the spring and autumn, and can have five or six babies per litter. This is obviously worth considering if you intend to keep a pair. You'll almost certainly be able to sell the babies to a pet shop or friends as pets, or to a very small disco as bouncers.

The hidden threat

The hidden threat is really in the fact that their bite is much worse than their bark which, when you consider that they don't bark at all, possibly isn't really saying much. But their bite is certainly worse than you'd expect from such a very cute animal. And that is their party piece – looking very cute, then taking the top off your finger!

Dog

What is it?

If the animal kingdom was relying on dogs to fight their corner, then they must by now be deeply disappointed. Dogs just don't do that sort of thing. Except pitbulls. Pitbulls will fight anything: corners, walls, doors, the lot. But not your average mutt. No – amazingly, dogs were about the first animal to catch on to the fact that if they made themselves useful, then Man would not eat them.

I say "amazingly" because dogs are universally stupid. Now you may say: "Oh, come on! That's a bit of a sweeping generalization! All dogs can't possibly be stupid!" Well, to that I reply: "Show me an intelligent dog, and I'll show you an actor in a skin."[1] Nonetheless, humans have long been unable to resist the animal known affectionately – and laughably, in my opinion – as Man's best friend.

What will it cost ?

As with most best friends, dogs do not come cheap.[2] Well, you can find them wandering aimlessly around in the streets, but if you want a pedigree one[3] then you could pay anything up to a few hundred pounds. It should really be at this point that common sense makes you say "why?" – but it never does.

1: This is ironic because actors are also notoriously stupid – except when they can con somebody into paying them millions of pounds to dress up and stand in front of a camera.
2: Or even go cheap for that matter. Or *cheep*.
3: Pedigree: this is the term used to denote any dog that has been given a really stupid name at birth.

Where will I keep it?

Some enterprising pet shop person years ago devised no end of doggie houses, beds, etc., which dog owners went out and spent their hard-earned cash on, only to discover that a dog will sleep anywhere other than in its basket/kennel.

What will it eat?

Since the time that Man and dog decided to share their domestic quarters, Rover has been used to sneaking under the dinner table and eating anything available: dropped food, swinging legs, etc. However, this is really not a good idea, especially if you want to be able to walk after your lunch.[1] Dogs should be fed special food – usually anything with Dog Food written on the tin – but not titbits.

1: Another way of making sure that you can still walk after your lunch is not to eat too much.

What will it do ?

The dog is the one animal that can be relied upon to make a fool of itself. This is in order to make you think that they really like you. It's not that difficult to understand. How often have you done something deeply embarrassing and cringe-making, just to persuade someone that you really like them? Often, I bet. And it never works, does it? Maybe you should really go for broke like dogs do and run after a stick.

RELAX, YOU'VE GOT THE JOB

Why do I want it ?

According to research – or rather, according to a vet who made a lot of money out of doing research and then writing a book about it[1] – pets, and especially dogs, are extremely good for us. They relieve stress, help us to exercise, and increase our life-expectancy. Well, I did a bit of checking on this vet and self-styled dog-expert, and I found out that he hasn't got a dog himself. I think the question we should be asking ourselves is: why not?

1: A book, incidentally, that I bought – thus adding to his ill-gotten fortune.

When will it die ?

Given proper care and attention, a dog can live for fifteen years or more. Some people use the old "seven dog years to every human year" theory to calculate when a dog is likely to die, but all that tells you is that some dogs die young. The most common cause of death for a dog is a traffic accident. This is because dogs are too stupid to be able to tell the difference between a car and a large stick on wheels.

Will it earn its keep ?

Some dogs have always been bred as working dogs. All this means is that they perform a natural function – chasing a stick – and the owner gets paid for it. Typical examples of this are:

Greyhound racing, where the stick is a mechanical rabbit;

Fox hounds, where the stick is a fox (or a horse's leg);

Gun dog, where the stick is a dead bird (or a gun);

Guard dog, where the stick is a burglar's leg (or worse!);

Guide dog, where the stick is hopefully anything other than a white stick.

Dogs have also traditionally been cross-bred for specific jobs. This involves mating dogs of different breeds in the hope of getting the best qualities of each breed fused in the finished article. This scheme has two basic drawbacks as far as I can see:

1) The chances of getting the best qualities of each breed, rather than the worst, are pretty remote.

2) Dogs don't have best qualities. They don't even have good qualities.

For some time now dog breeders have been trying to cross-breed a Labrador and a poodle for use as a guide dog. The new breed, called a Labradoodle, would be less prone to illness than its pure-bred counterpart, apparently. Unfortunately, during trials the dog kept detouring to the poodle-parlour, then sulking when its owner was unable to tell it how pretty it looked. Other cross-breeds in the pipeline include (apparently):

Old English Dachshund, bred as a more effective draught excluder;

Greyweiler, bred as a police dog that can catch a burglar and hang on to him until the police turn up;

Pittsu, small enough to go in your handbag/pocket, but great at preventing you from getting robbed.

What will I call it?

For some reason people insist on giving their dogs human names. I think this is all part of making them feel like a member of the family. There's really no need. A dog is the one animal who has ingratiated itself with humans to such a degree that it's hard to think of them as anything other than one of us. Don't. This is a mistake. A dog is a dog. Give it a dog's name. Like . . . er . . . oh, all right! Roger, then!

What else do I need to know?

Male dogs are called dogs, amazingly. Female dogs are called bitches, even the nice ones. Another way of making your animal earn its keep is to breed it. It isn't that difficult. If, for example, you want your bitch to have puppies, all you'll need is a dog and a Richard Clayderman record. But make sure your mutt is worth breeding. Any registered breeder will be pleased to advise you – and charge you a stud fee.

So far I have avoided suggesting that you should train

your dog to do tricks. This is time-consuming, frustrating and ultimately humiliating. But if you don't mind being humiliated then there have always been numerous outlets for talented pets, from *Star-Pets*, *Pets Win Prizes* through to the late *That's Life*. However, think very carefully before you take the plunge. Ask yourself: do I really want to get my pet too close to the likes of Peter Simon, Danny Baker or Esther Rantzen?

The hidden threat

I said earlier that all dogs are stupid, even though some of you will disagree with me. But don't be fooled into trying to prove me wrong. Don't, for instance, try and do anything even remotely intelligent with your mutt, because it will be doomed to failure. But it is exactly what other members of the animal kingdom want you to do. They want you to waste hours of your valuable time trying to turn your dog into a useful number of society – and failing. Believe me, I've tried it. Only the other day I tried to have a sensible conversation with my own dog. I talked slowly and added "ies" to the end of as many words as possible,[1] and actually I have to say that for a while I really felt that I was getting through. I was quite pleased with myself. I thought: maybe I'm wrong. Maybe dogs are quite bright after all. And after an hour or two of putting the world to rights in the company of my faithful friend, I turned away to leave the room, genuinely impressed and pleased with my achievement. And then the mutt went and spoiled it all by trying to sniff my bottom. No – a dog is a dog is a dog. It'll never be anything else!

1: As in *Bickies, Walkies, Antidisestablishmentarianismies*, etc.

HERE WITH ME TO DISCUSS THESE ISSUES ARE: EXPERT IN CULTURAL DYNAMICS, PROFESSOR ALEXANDER HERKINSMAUM; AUTHOR OF SINGULARITY IN PLURALISM, DR. OLIVER SPUTZ; LADY ELAINE FORFINGTON, DIRECTOR OF THE MULTI-REGIONAL AFFAIRS UNIT, AND BENGI.

TW IC

THE WORLD IN CRISIS

Elk

Elks, like other large cattle, don't actually make particularly good pets. However, having an elk in the house would mean that you always had somewhere to hang your hat.

Ferret

It's worth a mention in passing, as it is quite a popular domestic pet. The domestic ferret is a small carnivore, closely related to the polecat. The rarest ferret, the black-footed ferret, was until recently believed to be extinct. But some were found in Canada and the USA, bred in captivity, and released worldwide into the wild. Although mainly used by gamekeepers and poachers alike to catch rabbits, several in this country have recently broken into show business by taking part in the infamous "Ferret Down the Trouser-leg" stunt. As the name suggests, "performers" whose trousers have been secured at the ankles with string (or in more up-market exhibitions bicycle clips) will put a ferret down their trousers, a prize being awarded for the person (or ferret) who survives the longest. I am reliably informed that this is completely harmless, unless you happen to be wearing rabbit-flavoured underwear.

SPOT THE FERRET

Fish

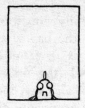

See **Goldfish/Tropical fish**

Frog

See **Tree frog**

Goldfish

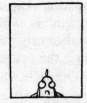

What is it?

Well, it used to be something you won at a fairground – the first step on the goldfish ladder to nowhere.

What will it cost?

Because winning the goldfish took six hundred goes and cost three years' pocket money, the goldfish assumed far greater importance than it ever deserved.

Gleefully you took it home in its plastic bag. You noticed the bag was leaky and so quickly transferred Goldie, as he was now called, to your mother's cut-glass fruitbowl (the only decent thing she got when she married, and that includes your father). Repeated ear-bashing eventually persuaded you to invest in a proper home for your new "friend". Is it my imagination, or is that furry patch on his side getting bigger?

Where will I keep it?

An aquarium – that's what you need. So you take yourself off to the pet shop, and return with all the necessary equipment: aquarium, gravel, weed, air-pump, a little plastic deep-sea diver[1] and one of those little Chinese bridges which for some strange reason fish fanciers obviously imagine litter the entire seabed.[2] The only thing the pet shop bloke didn't sell you was tap water, although he did try.

Proudly you set the whole thing up, fill it with water, and transfer Goldie to his new home. Your mum is extremely pleased that you have finally removed Goldie from the fruitbowl, because he had nibbled most of the apples.

1: This diver must be dead, because nobody could stay underwater that long.
2: Perhaps they do. I've never been down there. Maybe the Lost City of Atlantis is just a maze of Chinese takeaways.

What will it eat ?

Well, not apples, normally. Which only goes to show just how desperate Goldie has become. A normal goldfish diet would be anything that came in a small container with Goldfish Food written on the side. They do also eat ant eggs, so this is something to bear in mind if ever you're thinking of getting a second pet. But back to Goldie. Yes, that furry patch is definitely getting bigger.

What will it do ?

Swim around. Keep coming up to the glass wall of the aquarium and calling you Bob. Keep going up to the plastic diver to check that he's OK. Keep going up to the little Chinese bridge with a look of: "What the heck is that doing on the ocean bed?"

When will it die ?

In the case of Goldie, he will probably pop his clogs, even though fish don't wear clogs, within about ten minutes of you placing him in the (very expensive) aquarium. I knew that furry patch wasn't normal. But why should this be? Well, think about it. Poor Goldie (or whatever his or her real name is) has been living rough for months, travelling round the country, snatching a meal whenever he could. That's enough to give anybody a nasty furry patch. Look at the bloke who was running the side-show where you won him – didn't he have something very similar? I expect he'd be dead in *less* than ten minutes if you put him in an aquarium.

Will it earn its keep?

Not for you, certainly. But look at the amount of gold hanging off the various fingers of the side-show owner and judge for yourself. This is probably why he's not overworried about his own furry patch – he's probably a member of BUPA.

What will I call it?

In the case of Goldie, an expensive mistake. But one that – if you learn from it – will have been worth it. But you won't. You'll probably buy more. And the fish will then all call each other Bob. You might imagine that this would get confusing but, having no long-term memory, and therefore not remembering their own names, the fish probably never notice. Personally I think you should wait and see how their little personalities develop and name them accordingly. If you then find you end up with a tank full of fish called Boring, you could think again.

What else do I need to know?

Logic tells you that you now find yourself the proud owner of an empty aquarium. An empty aquarium isn't a lot of use, is it? Of course not! So what do you do? Advertise it for sale in the local paper and make a disgustingly large profit? Of course you don't! You do exactly what I did in the same situation. You say to yourself: "What I need is a new fish to replace Goldie. I was very fond of him, and miss him, even though he's buried in the back garden and I can go and talk to him whenever I want.[1] Besides, Goldie would want me to get a new fish." And so you do.

1: Unless the cat finds him first.

The hidden threat

Goldie is just a pawn in a much bigger game.[1] He is just a scaly link in an endless chain of dirty fishtanks. It is said that watching fish swimming around is very therapeutic. Watching other people's fish swimming around – safe in the knowledge that you'll never have to clean them out – probably is!

Gerbil

See **Mongolian Gerbil**

Golden hamster

The USA president John F Kennedy had two hamsters called Billy and Debby, but I don't think that's why he was shot.

What is it?

A hamster is a desert rodent, originally from Syria. It was introduced into Britain in 1931 for what my source-book called "laboratory work". I can only assume that this means cleaning and tidying up at night, because hamsters sleep during the day when all the real work would be going on. This puts hamsters into the category of nocturnal animals, which is another way of saying

1: Unlike Derek, who was just a prawn in a much bigger salad.

that they are very grumpy. It is very surprising to learn, therefore, that they still enjoy the position of being the nation's number one favourite pet.

What will it cost ?

A decent hamster will cost you around £5. I'm not sure what an indecent one will cost you, but this low price could account for their enormous popularity. They only cost a few pounds a month to feed, are quite clean and hardly any trouble. In fact if it wasn't for their bad temper they'd be the perfect pet.

Where will I keep it ?

A hamster cage, which will cost about £15. Hamsters are solitary animals, so make sure you get it a decent-sized one. The floor space should be at least half a square metre. Line the cage with a mixture of moss peat and straw, so that the hamster can burrow, and it's a good idea to add a solid hamster wheel. You can also get these plastic hamster balls, that the hamster goes inside and charges around the room in, but they are probably more fun for you than they are for the pet. He'd probably rather be sleeping.

What will it eat?

Obviously you can get special hamster food, but they also eat some fruit, vegetables and grasses.

What will it do?

Sleep. Rush about making a noise at night – when *you're* trying to sleep.

Why do I want it?

Probably because it is the most popular pet. It obviously waves some magic spell over people. But once they've got one, well . . .

When will it die?

I think it's significant that my research showed that the main cause of death in hamsters is old age, such is the risk-riddled life they lead. James Bond they are not. The average hamster will last two to three years, assuming it's well cared for and never gets involved in a traffic accident involving a hamster ball and a vacuum cleaner.

Will it earn its keep?

Not really, but it can probably be relied on to bite unwanted relatives or soon-to-be-unwanted boy/girlfriends. The trouble is very few hamsters can tell the difference between an unwanted relative, etc., and a wanted one. This is partly due to appalling eyesight, but mainly due to a deep-seated dislike of all humans.

What will I call it?

Hammy, Goldie (unless you've also got a fish). Frankly, whatever you call it, it is going to feel a deep sense of humiliation. Hamsters prefer to be aligned, in name at least, with the great solo achievers of this world. Sir Francis Chichester, Mother Theresa, Eddy "The Eagle" Edwards, even though they have no hope of achieving anything, except possibly the world sleeping record.

What else do I need to know?

There's nothing more I can tell you, but I feel sure that your hamster will leave you in no doubt as to your shortcomings as a guardian. Every look, waddle, and whisker twitch will cut you to the heart. And yet you'll still love him.

The hidden threat

Most animals realize that humans carry around a huge burden of guilt about what we are doing to *their* planet. None more so than the hamster. But he will suffer his lot in such a deafening silence that you will want to rush over to Syria and release him into the wild. Don't. For one thing he wouldn't survive five minutes, and for another he'd far rather live with you and make you feel sorry for him. As you approach his cage, he'll jump into the wheel and race around like someone demented, but his expression says: "I'm only doing this because I know it gives you pleasure."

Guinea pig

What is it?

If you see a large rat that looks like it's had an argument with a hairdrier, then it's probably a guinea pig. Their proper name is *Cavy*, and they were brought from South America by sailors in the 16th century. What I haven't been able to find out is why. Apparently they traded with the natives – a cavy for a few worthless beads. Personally, I think the sailors were robbed.

AND WHAT DID YOU GIVE THEM IN EXCHANGE FOR THIS ODD LITTLE BEAST?

PORTUGAL YOUR MAJESTY

What will it cost?

Being small and popular, guinea pigs sell for around £5. They are taken very seriously by guinea pig fanciers and there are a variety of different breeds that are recognized by their distinctive markings (*See illustration*).

DUTCH

PERUVIAN

HIMALAYAN

ABYSSINIAN

TORTOISESHELL

Where will I keep it?

Guinea pigs don't like being on their own, although if you keep two males together they'll probably fight. Two females, on the other hand, will live quite happily in a small rabbit hutch, as long as it's not full of rabbits. They also need plenty of exercise, so an outdoor run is a good idea, but make sure it's covered unless you want them to be attacked by dogs. Of course the other way to avoid this is not to let strange dogs into your back garden.

What will it eat?

Guinea pigs need large intakes of vitamin C, because – rather like humans – their bodies can't manufacture it or store it, but unlike humans they can't take high-dosage vitamin C tablets, mainly because they can't get the lid off the bottle. Good quality hay is also very important for them, as are all types of green vegetables: lettuce, cabbage, etc. They also like cereals and vegetable peelings, water and hot or cold milk.

What will it do ?

Well – eat, mostly. They are very keen eaters. This is partly due to the fact that they are greedy, but mainly because they can't do a lot else. Their little legs are too short for jumping or climbing, and they don't burrow. They don't even breed very much. So eating is about the only thing left, apart from sleeping, which they also do quite a bit of.

Why do I want it ?

Well, it's hard to say. They are not the most glamorous of pets, although you can show them.[1]

When will it die ?

Despite the fact that they don't involve themselves in any dangerous sports, like running or jumping, guinea pigs don't live very long – four to five years at the most. Still, that's probably about as much excitement as anyone can possibly take.

1: In fact you can show them practically anything – they probably won't be interested, especially if they're eating. Even more especially if they're sleeping.

Will it earn its keep?

Erm . . . no. Although obviously it would be quite easy to get it to sit for a portrait – either photographic or painted. All you need to do is find somebody stupid enough to want to pay to do it.

What will I call it?

Guinea pigs are good solid little animals that need good solid little names, like Porky.

What else do I need to know?

There used to be an old saying that if you picked a guinea pig up by its tail its eyes would pop out. Well, this is of course total nonsense. However, if you did pick him up by his tail he would probably die of shock – he hasn't got one.

The hidden threat

Although they are docile, guinea pigs look quite manic, as though they might suddenly do something alarming. And, who knows, they might. And that's the threat.

Horse

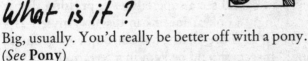

What is it?

Big, usually. You'd really be better off with a pony. (*See* **Pony**)

HORSE   PONY

House cricket

Unlike bush crickets, house crickets actually thrive in captivity, so you wouldn't have to keep releasing them every few days. But – wouldn't you know it? – they are virtually impossible to catch, and because they've got wings they keep flying away! That's Pet Power for you!

Insect

Insects can be pets too. Even the humble stick insect. Well, I say "humble" but a stick insect is anything but. If you were to hold a very powerful magnifying glass up to his face, you would see a supercilious expression that is clearly saying: "Look at me! I can disguise myself as a stick! Which is more than you can do, you great fat pudding!" Insects should be kept in a terrarium. As you know, these are explained later in the book.

Jumbuck

Apart from it appearing in the Australian National Anthem, "Waltzing Matilda", I have no idea what they are, although I do know that they are very popular with "swagmen" who eventually end up doing something illegal to them – according to the song.

Kestrel

Keeping birds of prey is a very specialized field. In fact you'll need a very specialized field to fly them in, because they do need a lot of exercise. However, if it's something you're interested in it's worth finding out more from a local expert. Incidentally, most birds of prey like eating mice. I don't know whether this would help to solve any other pet problems.

Lion

What is it?
A totally unsuitable pet.

What will it cost?
An arm and a leg.

Where will I keep it?
It'll decide that.

What will it eat?
Your relatives.

What will it do?
Eat your other relatives.

Why do I want it?
Because you've got a lot of unwanted relatives?

When will it die?
When there are no relatives left to eat.

Will it earn its keep ?

Not unless you can corner the market in getting rid of
unwanted relatives.

WHAT DO YOU MEAN YOU'RE
OUT OF RELATIVES...YOU'RE
RELATED TO YOUR MOTHER
AREN'T YOU ?

What will I call it ?

Hungry.

What else do I need to know ?

The name of a good doctor.

The hidden threat

That it might forget that you're its owner, and think
you're its lunch.

Mice

What is it ? (sorry — are they?)

Small members of the rodent family. At one time mice
were very popular as small pets. But, like gerbils, they
are smelly and take some looking after. But they are
cheap. Strangely enough mice were once used in
numerous experiments to help solve all manner of
earth-shattering problems. Which probably explains
why these problems are still with us today.

What will they cost ?

You can buy mice for as little as 75p. In fact I found one shop that was giving two away to anyone who bought a cage. Why anyone would want to buy a cage without thinking about what they were going to have in it first, I don't know, but still!

Where will I keep them ?

In a cage. In fact go to the pet shop mentioned above, and they'll already be in there. Line the cage with hay or wood shavings. Don't use sawdust, because this gets up their nose.[1]

1: Unless of course you want to get up their nose.

What will they eat?

Not cheese. This is something that was dreamt up by somebody in Hollywood – after eating too much cheese, probably. They like oats, wholemeal bread, fruit and bird seed. Canary seed is best because it contains high-fat crops like rape, linseed and hemp. But don't overdo the canary seed, otherwise you might find that when you open the cage your mice fly off.

What will they do?

Sniff inquisitively, mostly. They quite like wheels, because they're not bright enough to realize that they're getting nowhere.

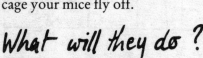

When will they die?

Sadly, mice, like many of the small rodents, have very poor recuperative powers. Which – in simple language – means that if they get ill they usually don't get better.[1] Which also means that they don't live long at all. No sooner have you started to say: "Phew! Those mice smell!" than they've died.[2]

1: I know, because I looked it up!
2: It could be this that's making them smell, of course!

Will they earn their keep?

No. At one time you could sell them to pet shops and at least recoup the cost of keeping them, but now even the pet shops don't want them. In fact one shop I went into said they feel so sorry for people bringing in baby mice that they give them a free bag of food!

What will I call them?

Nibbler, Squeaker, anything that suggests something small and noisy in a high-pitched sort of way.

What else do I need to know?

Mice are very smelly, unless you clean their cage very regularly. In fact they're very smelly even if you do.

The hidden threat

It's just possible that the mice who took part in all those tests and experiments in order to prove or disprove some mathematical theory, but proving instead that mice are stupid – it's just possible that the mice failed because they wanted to. That in fact they are extremely intelligent life forms. Hard to accept, I agree, but possible. It's also possible that, given this superior intelligence, they are all just waiting for the signal to take over the world!

Mongolian gerbil

What is it?

The Mongolian gerbil, or Yellow Rat, is a small rodent that was originally captured for use in laboratory experiments. You know the kind of thing: "What will happen if we squirt shampoo into a gerbil's eye?" This research enables scientists to publish papers with titles like: "What *did* happen when I squirted shampoo into a gerbil's eye". Well, I suppose it makes a change from "What I did on my holidays". What these scientists don't realize is that a gerbil never forgets.

What will it cost?

Gerbils are best kept in pairs. A boy and a girl is best, particularly if you want to breed them, and not have them trying to kill each other 24 hours a day. A breeding pair will cost around £7–10. They'll probably have up to nine litters of six to eight babies at a time which, if you are lucky, you'll be able to sell to friends or to a pet shop. (*See section on Earning Their Keep!*)

Where will I keep it?

Gerbils do like to run about a lot, so they need a decent-sized cage (another tenner!) You can put sand in the cage, but don't bother with a bucket and spade, as they'll be too busy dashing about.

What will it eat?

If they can't get anything else – the end of your finger. Gerbils can give a very painful bite, so make sure they have a good supply of nuts, seeds, bits of fruit and so on instead. You can of course buy proper gerbil food, which saves you the bother of mixing stuff up, but be warned – gerbils are quite fussy eaters.[1]

1: They won't bite just anybody. It'll always be the one person you least want them to bite. Like you!

What will it do ?

Apart from biting and running about . . . er . . . nothing. You'll find those two activities take up all their waking hours.

DING DING DING DING
DING
DING
DING

ANOTHER BUSY DAY OF BITING AND RUNNING ABOUT

When will it die ?

Well, they can live for about three years, after which time your fingers will have a chance to heal properly.

Will it earn its keep ?

If you breed them and you can sell the babies, then I suppose they might just pay for their food, because they aren't that expensive in the first place, However, you can put your gerbil's biting obsession to good use. A gerbil can demolish an entire newspaper quicker than the average person can read it,[1] so they do have great potential in today's world where recycling is the name of the game. A quick word with your local supermarket could lead to you being able to set up a gerbil recycling plant next to the bottle bank. A couple of gerbils could probably shred an entire town's old newspapers, ready for pulping, in an afternoon. But before you get too excited, check the hidden threat.

1: Except the *Sun*, obviously.

What will I call it?

With pets like gerbils people often favour a bit of alliteration, as in Jerry the Gerbil, Georgina the Gerbil and so on. I think Genghis would be more suitable.

What else do I need to know?

Nothing much. Oh, they are very smelly, and require a lot of "cleaning out" – that's Gerbil-speak for "people sticking their finger in our cage". Just never forget, when you're doing this, why they were originally brought to this country. They certainly haven't!

The hidden threat

Before you offer your gerbils' services as a recycling plant, you should remind yourself of the fact that gerbils can be extremely unpredictable in the area of finger-biting. You could easily find that, although you might get paid handsomely for your recycling efforts, you could also be paying out for huge hospital bills for the various unsuspecting people providing the raw materials.[1]

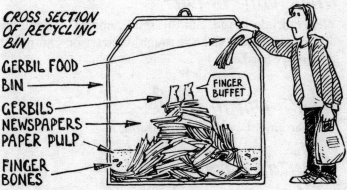

CROSS SECTION OF RECYCLING BIN

GERBIL FOOD BIN →

GERBILS →

NEWSPAPERS PAPER PULP →

FINGER BONES →

FINGER BUFFET

1: Newspapers and fingers.

Nits

This is the common term for that school favourite, the head louse.

What is it?

Well, it's not really a pet, although several people keep them, usually unwittingly.

What will it cost?

Nothing. You can pick them up almost anywhere.

Where will I keep it?

On your head.

What will it eat?

Well, it drinks blood. But this is no vampire, so don't try driving a wooden stake through its heart or you might get a nasty headache.

What will it do?

Walk around. Lay eggs. Drink blood.

Why do I want it?

Well, you probably don't really.

When will it die?

Shortly after you wash your hair in this really revolting and expensive shampoo.

Will it earn its keep?

Not unless you've invested your hard-earned cash in shares in The Really Revolting and Expensive Shampoo Company.

What will I call it?

All manner of names spring to mind, but none of them are really fit to print here.

What else do I need to know?

That they've only come to visit because they really like you – you have such beautifully clean hair.

The hidden threat

Like a lot of animals, nits have had a really bad press, and so I suppose the only threat is that people believe the old wives' tale that if you've got nits then you must be filthy. Although of course you might well be!

Nocturnal pet

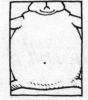

These are really a bit of a waste of time! (*See* **Golden hamster**)

Overweight pets

It is very cruel to your pet to overfeed it. Another good way to be cruel to it is to dress it up in silly clothes, or take it to a bonfire party.[1]

Parrot

What is it?

Very, very noisy. And vicious. And bad tempered. Still fancy one? Then read on! In the course of researching this book, I went into a pet shop which had a parrot. I knew it had a parrot, because from about a kilometre

1: Don't contact the RSPCA – I'm not actually suggesting you do either of these things!

down the road I could hear this noise that sounded like someone being tortured by the Spanish Inquisition. But, having become a bit of an expert, I could tell it was actually "Pretty Polly". On entering the shop, sure enough I saw the cage, with a sign saying "Parrot – £500 – may bite". Apparently for £750 it would have taken my arm off! So what is the attraction of these birds? Well they are colourful, as is their language. They are also quite romantic, being traditionally associated with pirates and treasure. I suppose that the most famous one is Long John Silver's parrot, Captain Flint. It's only when you get to know a parrot that you realize why Long John Silver only had one leg!

What will it cost ?

They are expensive. Put it this way, there are cheaper ways of getting unwanted limbs removed.[1] An average parrot will cost around £300, although they tend to have to be sold in a cage[2], which puts the price up to around £500.

1: The National Health Service, for instance. Although there is a six-year waiting list. This is because they use a parrot, and they only have the one.
2: You can't take them home in a paper bag.

Where will I keep it ?

In a cage, as I've just mentioned. It should be large and strong. It is also a good idea to make the door lockable. Electrifying the bars is not a bad idea. (OK, maybe not!)

What will it eat ?

Seeds. Sunflower seeds are very popular with most parrots, mainly because they can give you a nasty cut if they hit you in the back of the neck. They also like fruit, and anything that stains clothing.

What will it do ?

There's nothing a parrot likes more than to pick up the aforementioned sunflower seed and bounce it off the back of an important guest's head. Then, because they are great talkers, they'll say something like: "The vicar threw it." Since the vicar is there and since the parrot was able to mimic the one person in the room whom everyone knows never lies, this naturally causes trouble, and in the ensuing punch-up, the parrot will offer its services as a mercenary maimer to anyone fool enough to open the cage. Basically parrots thrive on trouble.

Why do I want it?

This is the unanswerable question, I'm afraid. Although I have met parrot-owners who are perfectly happy. Scarred, with limbs missing and no friends, but perfectly happy.

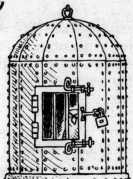

When will it die?

Not nearly soon enough, I'm afraid. Parrots live for a very long time, 90 years in some cases. This is mainly because they can – to paraphrase Rudyard Kipling[1] – keep their heads while all around are losing theirs and blaming it on anybody but the parrot, even though the parrot probably started the trouble in the first place.

Will it earn its keep?

In the unlikely event of your parrot actually liking you, I suppose it might be possible to make money hiring it out to people so that they can use it to annoy their neighbours, but this would not be a good reason to get one. A good reason to get one would be . . . er . . . sorry! I can't think of one!

What will I call it?

For some reason people seem to call parrots "Polly". This is a definite mistake, and could explain some of the anger parrots obviously feel towards humans. The name Polly suggests somebody – a girl usually – who is small

---

1: Or should that be "parrot-phrase"?

and pretty and put-upon: Little Polly Flinders, Polly put the kettle on, etc. Parrots are just not Pollys, sorry. Nosher, Killer, Big Eric – these are far more suitable. But never Polly!

YOU TELL ME, WHO *IS* A PRETTY BOY THEN ?

What else do I need to know ?

I can't think of anything. If you've continued reading this entry this far, you've probably already made your mind up about parrots and you just want to see what I think, even thought you probably don't agree. Please yourself, but never say that I didn't warn you.

The hidden threat

The one good thing about parrots is that there is no hidden threat. If they don't like you – which they probably won't – you will be left in no doubt. And probably in no fit state to hold a pencil.

Pony

What is it ?

The term pony has come to refer to any small horse, although this isn't strictly accurate. Still, when have I ever let a little thing like accuracy get in the way of my writing? Basically, a pony is a small horse (less than 14 hands), and that's that. It is also not a pet to take on lightly (however many hands you've got), especially if you don't like riding.

What will it cost ?

This is also not a pet that you can expect to pay for out of your pocket money, unless of course your parents own half of Hampshire. Keeping a pony is a tricky and expensive business, and boy, won't your pony let you know it if you cut any corners. The pony itself will probably cost you between £600 and £2,000. You can get ponies for about 40p, but then they tend to be in tins marked Dog Food.

Where will I keep it ?

On top of the cost of the animal you'll also have to consider this carefully, unless of course you already live in a field. Ponies need to be properly stabled. No, you can't keep them in your bedroom! I have seen stabling advertised locally at around £12.50 per week. I assume this is about average, although it probably varies amazingly from area to area.

What will it eat?

Grass. But before you think "Great! I'll just let it run around on next-door's lawn!", it is really not that simple. Things never are where animals are concerned. Because ponies have very small stomachs (even though they are often quite podgy), they need access to food all the time, so that they can eat little and often. They also need good quality hay, oats, barley and maize. This often comes in the form of Pony Nuts, which are just pony convenience food.

You see, we're all at it, even the animals! The cost of food may well be included in the cost of stabling, although I wouldn't bank on it. Ponies are heavy drinkers – about 36 litres a day! But because it's only water it never really develops into a serious drink problem.

What will it do?

Ponies do need a lot of exercise. So apart from eating, they'll do a lot of running around. Obviously riding is good exercise for them – as well as for you.

Why do I want it?

The main reason people have ponies is to ride them. Obviously there are some people who have ponies so that they can say *I've got a pony, you know*, but this is very rare. So, assuming that you've got a pony to ride, you'll also need the proper gear, and this is where the cost starts to escalate, unless you're very careful. To ride a pony you'll need the following:

ITEM	APPROXIMATE COST
Saddle	£300 – £450
Bridle, bit, irons, girth	£100 – £200
Pony rug	£30 – £100
Miscellaneous (brushes etc)	£50 – £100
Tube of Superglue*	£1.75

* This is to keep you in the saddle.

Apart from all this stuff, you will also need to dress the part. So you'll need:

ITEM	APPROXIMATE COST
Riding hat	£20 – £30
Jodphurs (Not essential)	£18 – £25
Boots	£20 – £30

You will also need expert tuition, because riding a pony is a complicated business. Just getting on is hard enough, never mind staying on! You can expect to pay £5 for each riding lesson. You can expect to pay it, but you'll probably find that they cost nearer £10! But make sure you get the best lessons available in your area. Obviously if you can get lessons at the stables where your pony is kept then that would make the most sense, so shop around. But – as you can see – it is an expensive pet, and so you must be totally convinced that riding is what you want to do. A lot of people think they want to ride, get all the stuff, and then realize that they don't like it. In fact this happens quite often. The only good thing about that is it means that you might be able to find a pony "going cheap".[1] But a word of warning: make sure that the reason they gave up riding their pony wasn't because it was unrideable – or stuffed.

When will it die?

If properly taken care of, a healthy pony can live for many years, 20–25 in fact, but they do take a lot of looking after. Because they are out of doors a lot, and with other ponies, they catch all sorts of things, so you can add the cost of vet's bills to the list of expenses.

1: A pony "going cheap" is fine. But if it's going cheep-cheep, don't buy it. It's probably a budgie.

Will it earn its keep?

Not really, although if you get good enough you can enter riding or jumping competitions, where you might, if you're lucky enough (and good enough), win cash prizes, which would help feed the animal. Mind you, you're probably far more likely to win a non-edible rosette!

What will I call it?

Any name ending in "y" or "er" seems to be popular. Find a name to suit your animal. Grumpy or Sulker would suit most ponies.

What else do I need to know?

Ponies are very highly strung and sensitive, or so they'd have you believe.

Probably because of this they wet the bed a lot, and need constant "mucking out". Of course the stables might do this as part of the fee, but they aren't really too happy if you only ever turn up to ride the thing. So think hard about whether you want to spend most of your free time wearing wellingtons and smelling like an allotment before you take on this particular pet.

The hidden threat

Ponies do like a lot of attention. And if they don't get it, they have ways of making you pay. Like refusing to move, or making you fall off – so be warned!

Queen bee

See **Bee**

Rabbit

What is it ?

Well, it's not a little fluffy bundle for a start. They are fluffy, certainly. They are also cute-looking, but looks can be very deceptive. And in the case of the rabbit, they always are.

What will it cost ?

A rabbit can cost you anything from £5 to £15 (or more). This obviously depends on the pedigree. A Butcher's Rabbit, one originally bred for meat, will cost less and live longer, with the added attraction that you can eat him if you get bored with him.

A BUTCHER'S RABBIT | A BUTCHER RABBIT

£3 per Kilo

Where will I keep it ?

A hutch. Rabbits need three square metres of hutch floor space per animal. They also need separate night and day quarters, with the night quarters taking up about a third of the total space. The reason they need these separate areas is because rabbits get bored very easily, and they quite like to nip into the night area and back out again and pretend that it's tomorrow. As you can imagine, rabbits are also pretty stupid. They also need an exercise area, about twice the size of their living quarters. But remember to sink the netting below ground level, because rabbits can burrow. If all this is making you say:

"Well, a rabbit's no good – I live in a flat!" it may interest you to know that more and more people are keeping rabbits in the house, and letting them run around the floor. It is apparently quite easy to domesticate a rabbit. But before you get too excited just remember that you can't teach rabbits to talk, so he's never going to be able to ask you to lift him on to the toilet when he wants to "go".

What will it eat?

Well, it's not a carrot chomper, that's the first thing. This image, mainly encouraged by the makers of Bugs Bunny cartoons, of a rabbit nibbling a carrot is quite wrong. For a start rabbits originate from Spain. So, instead of going: "What's up, Doc?", Bugs should actually be saying: "What's Up With Paella All Of A Sudden?" Not that they eat paella – they don't. No, they are grazing animals, so they eat grass, hay, oats, grain, etc. You can of course buy specially balanced rabbit "convenience" food. Alternatively you could buy one of those free-standing rabbit runs that you move around the lawn.

What will it do?

Well, it will do all the things that cartoon rabbit creators would have you believe it will do, apart from talk, dress up, or in fact anything even vaguely intelligent. But it will twitch its nose and hop, and look fluffy. It will also kick and bite, so be careful.

Why do I want it?

Well, I suppose most people have rabbits because they are cute and fluffy, even if they aren't anything like as cuddly as you might imagine. My family has a rabbit that will climb on your knee and cuddle up to you like a small child, which is quite pleasant. But then it will suddenly, and for no apparent reason, go for your throat. It's quite a conversation stopper, particularly if the person cuddling it is doing the talking at the time.

When will it die?

If you keep it well fed and cared for, a rabbit will live for around eight years. A Butcher's Rabbit will last for 15 years, particularly if he shares a home with a family of vegetarians.

Will it earn its keep?

No. It's a domestic pet. Although I have, I think, hit on a brilliant way of making him a good earner, as well as reducing his boredom, for which I think you'll find him extremely grateful – particularly if you whisper the magic words "rabbit pie" into his ear occasionally. What you'll need is a free-standing rabbit run. You mount this on wheels and add a small solar-powered motor to the back, put Bunny inside, and you now have the first totally environmentally-friendly lawn mower. Bunny will eat the grass, as the motor drives the run up and down the lawn. Careful adjustment of the motor's speed, plus a little well-regulated starving of the rabbit beforehand, should ensure that you cut an average-sized lawn in a matter of minutes. By using more than one rabbit you could probably do an entire street in an afternoon. In just a few weeks you could become the Richard Branson or Anita Roddick of the lawn-mowing world. And Bunny would have no time to get bored.

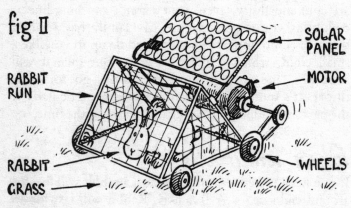

fig II

SOLAR PANEL

MOTOR

RABBIT RUN

RABBIT

WHEELS

GRASS

What will I call it?

Rabbits cry out to be called things like Fluffy and Hoppitty. Well they don't actually. Actually they probably don't care what you call them, as long as you don't call them Lunch.

What else do I need to know?

It's an old wives' tale that you should pick a rabbit up by its ears. You really shouldn't do it. In fact you really shouldn't pick them up at all, unless you know they like it. There is one sure way to find this out: pick them up.

If they kick, bite, wriggle and scratch, you know that they don't!

The hidden threat

As I mentioned earlier, you can domesticate a rabbit. Why anyone would want to bother is another matter, but it can be done. You can in fact even teach them to use a cat-litter tray. A cat-flap even! Now, before you start getting excited at this prospect, take a look at your pet dog. You welcomed him into your home, didn't you? You treated him as one of the family, didn't you? And where is he now sleeping? I rest my case!

Rat

What is it ?

A rodent. The cleanest, friendliest and most delightful pet you could ever hope to "own". At least that's what I was told when I enquired. Admittedly the person who told me had a pointed nose, cute little ears and a long tail, but why shouldn't I believe her?

What will it cost ?

Rats are best kept in pairs, but don't mix the sexes unless you want to be over-run with them! Two male rats will live quite happily together, especially if they are together from a young age, before they have met any females. Never mix one female with two males, unless you want to spend all your spare time settling arguments, dealing with petty jealousies and counselling jilted boyfriends.

They should cost around £2.50. If you're charged much more than that, then it's probably because the rat is getting a percentage of the fee.

Where will I keep it?

In a cage. Since rats gnaw, a metal one is best. Make sure it's large enough – 75cm × 30cm × 30cm high per pair of rats. Put in things for your rats to climb on or crawl through. Line it with sawdust and bits of newspaper. That way, if they get bored climbing and tunnelling, they can have a bit of a read.

What will it eat?

Oats, nuts, etc. Go for anything with Rat Food on the bag. Avoid anything with Rat Poison on the bag.

What will it do?

Tunnel, climb, sleep. What it won't do is spread the Black Death, or go chasing after the first bloke who comes along dressed in a party-coloured suit playing a tin whistle. This is the rat of yesteryear. The modern rat has cleaned up his act quite considerably.

Why do I want it?

Rats, despite everything you may believe about them, are friendly, clean, like being handled, and are good fun.

When will it die?

Unfortunately this good fun is very short-lived. Rats have a short life-span, about three or four years – just long enough for you to get really attached to it and for Michael Jackson to write a song about it.

Will it earn its keep?

Well, if you bred them, I'm sure you'd be able to sell them, to a pet shop or friends. They can have as many as a dozen babies per litter, but when you consider that they are quite cheap to buy anyway, your poor rats would have to have an awful lot of babies before you made your first million. It's certainly not worth giving up your education for.

What will I call it?

Ben. Next question.

The hidden threat

As I have said, rats are very friendly. But they can afford to be. They are one of the few animals that were feared by man and not exploited. So they know that, ultimately, they have the upper hand, because you'll never know whether all those stories about them carrying the Black Death are true, until you catch it, by which time you'll be a gibbering wreck anyway.

Snail

What is it?

Usually the first course in a French restaurant. Although these are not common English garden snails, so don't try boiling some up for tea, because they are not edible! Garden snails make a useful addition to your terrarium, and get along well with other small creatures.

JAN	FEB	MAR	APR	MAY	JUNE

What will it cost ?

Nothing. They are easy to catch in the garden, particularly at night when it's damp.

Where will I keep it ?

Well, in your terrarium. You can keep it in your pocket, but I certainly wouldn't recommend it!

What will it eat ?

Snails eat leaves. As with caterpillars, try and get some of the leaves he was on when you caught him, as these are probably his favourite.

What will it do ?

Move around very slowly leaving a slimy trail and . . . er . . . that's it, really.

Why do I want it ?

As a pet on its own I must admit that I can't really think of any good reason for keeping a snail, but as part of a menagerie in a terrarium, then I think he's worth having.

JULY	AUG	SEP	OCT	NOV	DEC
					AND STAY OUT!

When will it die?

I'm honestly not sure. The ones in my garden usually die when I accidentally step on them when I go out there with the dog at night. But – although it's sad – there are plenty more.

Will it earn its keep?

No. Although you'll be doing your garden a favour by keeping it off the flowerbeds.

What will I call it?

Slimy springs to mind. Can't think why.

What else do I need to know?

They are basically pests. So be careful where you put them if you get fed up with them in your terrarium. Don't, for instance, put them back among the flowers.

The hidden threat

It's just possible that snails have a highly developed sense of humour. And if this is so it's just possible that they are having the last laugh. That in fact they are edible, and we don't realize it.

So we pay a fortune to eat French ones in restaurants, when in fact we could be barbecuing our own. Well, even if it's true, I for one am not going to try it!

NON NON! YOU ARE MAKING UN TERRIBLE MISTAKE GUV!

Snake

What is it?

If it wraps itself around you and squeezes and squeezes until you die, then it's probably a Boa Constrictor. If it lies there doing nothing, then it's probably a piece of string. Snakes are extremely expensive and specialized pets, and are not to be taken on lightly. However, they do make good pets, and are useful for threatening smaller brothers or sisters into getting them to tidy your room, so if you're interested in having a snake you'd be well advised to consult a real expert.

Spider

What is it?

Spiders come in many different types and sizes, although they all have one thing in common – they have far too many legs!

What will it cost?

This depends entirely on where you get your spider. The ones in the bath cost nothing. The ones from the pet shop can cost anything up to £50. That would be for a large tarantula. If you're going for the bathroom variety, don't get the one actually in the bath – he's probably a male on the lookout for a female. He'd heard that there were these really leggy females hanging round the pool, so he thought he'd drop in. Ignore him, unless you want to try and mate him with your female. You'll find her in a web, unless your house is exceptionally tidy!

Where will I keep it?

Transfer her to your terrarium, and watch her set up home there.

What will it eat?

Well – in the case of the house spider – if you do try and mate your female, she'll eat the male, either before or after they've mated. Other than that you should feed her live flies. Why live? Well, female spiders have terrible eyesight,[1] so they won't know that the fly is there unless they feel it land on the web. You could try banging a dinner gong, but I don't think they hear too well either! Tarantulas, incidentally, won't thank you for a measly fly! They prefer crickets (*See also* **Bush/House Cricket**), or the odd locust.

What will it do?

Make a web, eat flies, eat male spiders, lay eggs, er . . . that's it.

I GOT SICK OF SPINNING WEBS, SO I SPUN MYSELF A THREE PIECE SUITE

1: Let's face it they'd have to have to fancy a male spider!

Why do I want it?

Well, I suppose so that you can watch it make a web, eat flies, eat male spiders, lay eggs, er . . . that's it really.

When will it die?

Tarantulas live for about one year in captivity. I'm really not sure about house spiders, but the male certainly lives a lot longer by avoiding going on heavy dates!

Will it earn its keep?

No. Not unless you think can make money by offering to rid your neighbourhood of flies.[1]

What will I call it?

Incey-Wincey? That might suit a house spider. It's rather too twee for a tarantula.

What else do I need to know?

In the case of tarantulas and the like you would be advised to talk to an expert. That – as I am sure you've guessed – is not me!

The hidden threat

Spiders, however small, have one big thing running in their favour. One thing that means they command respect wherever they care to go, even in the bath. And that is the fact that lots and lots of people are frightened of them, usually without good reason!

1: Don't even bother offering to rid your neighbourhood of locusts. We don't have many swarms of locusts in this country!

Terrapin

Not a suitable pet for a child, as you can catch salmonella from them. Because of this small children often mistake them for hamburgers.

Tortoise

These are now extremely rare, and therefore not a popular pet. This could be due to an import ban that was placed on them forcing the price up, but I think it's more likely that people simply got fed up with them running away. I know I did with mine. "Running away?" I hear you exclaim. "Yes!" I reply. "Running away!" "But tortoises move very very very slowly," I hear you counter. "They do – when you're looking."

CROSS SECTION OF TORTOISE

VISIBLE EVERYDAY LEGS

HIDDEN RACING LEGS

I'll never ever forget the hundreds of times I was watching my pet tortoise (er . . . whatever his name was) struggling across the garden and thinking "I wonder if it would help to paint Go-faster stripes on his shell". Then

I would be distracted for literally a split second (usually by another pet, come to think of it). And when I turned back – blimey! Erm . . . whatsisname was a hundred metres and four gardens away, chomping on Mr Wayne's prize lettuce. How did he do it? He must have run, unless a passing sparrow had air-lifted him there. It used to drive me mad! Which, of course, is why . . . er . . . Thingy did it. And it did no good shouting at him, he was very thick skinned.

Tree frog

What is it?

Unlike ordinary frogs, these chaps spend their days climbing trees – hence the name! But don't start looking up your local elm, you won't find any. You'll need to visit your local pet shop.

What will it cost?

Some can cost as much as £30.

Where will I keep it?

In a terrarium. They need plenty of moisture for their skin, and obviously bits of tree to climb.

What will it eat?

Flies, crickets, that sort of thing. The large ones will even tackle a baby mouse!

What will it do?

As the name suggests, it will spend quite a bit of time climbing trees. But they do like having a swim, so some water in your terrarium would be a good idea.

Why do I want it?

I don't know – why DO you want it?

When will it die?

Some of them can live quite long – eight to ten years. So be sure you want him in the first place!

Will it earn its keep?

No. Not unless tree-climbing suddenly becomes an Olympic sport.

What will I call it ?

Whatever you like. They won't understand because they don't speak English very well. They mostly come from Australia.

What else do I need to know ?

Tree frogs are really toads. They can move their heads to look at flies. Frogs can't do that. They can also sing. But having heard other Australian singers, such as Jason and Kylie, you probably won't want to encourage them!

The hidden threat

As far as I can tell, there isn't one. But to me that just makes matters worse! That is Pet Power at its most alarming!

Tropical fish

What is it ?

Well, it's a fish normally found in tropical waters, but now found in any good pet shop or garden centre that stocks tropical fish. The tell-tale sign to look for is a sign in the window saying: "We stock tropical fish".

What will it cost ?

As with many pets, the actual cost of the animal isn't the greatest expense. Although tropical fish can cost as much as £2,000, you can pick one up for less than fifty pence. Mind you, you'll probably need a microscope to see him, and he'll look pretty silly swimming around in a huge aquarium. But at least he's cheap!

Where will I keep it ?

Oh, sorry! I thought I'd just told you – a huge aquarium. That's what you'll need if you are going to keep this particular pet properly. No fruit bowl for this geezer, even the best one! (*See also* **Goldfish**) Because he's tropical (even if he was actually born in Chelmsford) he'll want heated water and an undergravel air pump. That's what he's used to. Why do you think people go to the tropics for their holidays? Well, it doesn't need to be that huge, but because tropical fish are something you can collect, like stamps,[1] then you should try to calculate how large a tank you think you might need eventually. Obviously fish tanks are not things you can easily build on to, unlike hamster houses. (*See also* **Golden Hamsters**.) The way to calculate this is to decide roughly how many fish you'd like to end up with eventually, taking into account the odd one sent through the post by batty relatives,[2] then allow 10 square centimetres per centimetre of fish. How do you calculate this? Lay all your fish out on a sheet of paper and measure them. No, not really! Guess. A proper tank will cost around £100. You'll need to leave it switched on and standing for two to four weeks before you add any fish or plants. But obviously you put the water in! After this time you can start adding your fish.

1: I think there is probably one that looks exactly like a stamp. It may even be sticky on one side.
2: This is a joke. I think it's actually illegal to send fish through the post, even dead ones.

What will it eat?

It really depends which tropical fish you've got. The best thing is to take advice from the shop where you bought them. Also take advice when selecting your fish, otherwise you may find that the thing they like eating most is each other!

What will it do?

Well, surprisingly enough, fish tend to swim around a lot. And more than likely that's what yours will do. Of course they might try standing perfectly still for hours on end just to worry you, but take no notice – pets are like that. It's only when they lie on the surface of the water for weeks doing absolutely nothing that you know something is definitely up. Fish have an extremely short-term memory – a matter of minutes – and so they would never be able to remember that they were playing you up for this length of time.

When will it die?

Any time. This is the trouble with tropical fish. The slightest thing can give them a disease, and this will wipe out the whole tank.

122

Will it earn its keep?

No. Next question.

What will I call it?

Tropical fish are so small (some of them anyway), that it's quite difficult to tell them apart. But I think that when you realize that they are already have names like: *Pearl Gourami, Plecostomus, Shubunkins, Corydoras, Pangasius, Zebra Danio* and *Rosy Barb* – all names incidentally forced on them by Man – then I think you'll agree that they've already got enough to cope with, without being called Derek as well!

What else do I need to know?

Lots, I expect. I spent an hour in a fish shop talking to the owner, who really knew his onions. It was then that I realized that I was in the wrong kind of fish shop. Still, he got an offer of a signed copy of this book out of it, and I got a saveloy.

The hidden threat

It's the dying thing, really. Fish seem to have an uncanny knack of knowing when you've just stretched yourself to your financial limits. You've taken on your ninth paper round, promised your body to the sixth form for experimentation, or worse. It is at this point that they all up and die on you, leaving you with a huge aquarium that no one will touch with a barge-pole, mainly because fish have recently died in it. This is a more kamikaze element of the Pet Power strategy, but it works every time.

Ugly pet

UGLY PET
(OR ITS OWNER)

There is no doubt that some pets are amazingly ugly. But since pets tend to look like their owners I would be careful who you say this to!

Viper

VIPER
(OR GRASS SNAKE)

Is not a good pet. In the wild it often gets mistaken for a grass snake. This is not a healthy mistake to make. The way to tell the difference is that one of them has a bite that can kill, and the other one doesn't. I don't suggest you use this as a test to find out which one you've got hold of!

Worm

What is it ?

A wriggly brown thing about 10 cm long. There are also

124

paler, shorter, fatter ones – these are the ones to get. The big brown ones make better breakfasts for the wild birds in your garden.

What will it cost ?

Nothing. Your garden is probably full of them. Unless you've only got a window box.

Where will I keep it ?

Worms are great in a terrarium constructed to suit them. Put in plenty of damp earth and scatter dead plants, old leaves and garden stuff on top.

What will it eat?

The leaves and garden stuff. What else?

What will it do?

Once it has digested the leaves and so on, they will come out at the other end – you're not reading this at the dinner table, are you? Good! – and fill the soil in your terrarium with nutrients and goodness.

Why do I want it?

Ah, well you see this is the whole point! In a very short time the soil in your terrarium will be so rich in nutrients that any half-decent gardener would kill to get his hands on it.

When will it die?

Oh, don't worry about that! There's plenty more where he came from!

Will it earn its keep?

Yes! That is, if you can persuade the eager gardener that this nutrient-rich soil is worth paying for! This might be a bit tricky with your dad, because he might retaliate by charging you for using his worms!

What will I call it?

Don't bother. These worms are working for you, and it doesn't pay to get too friendly with the workers. I wouldn't even bother to have a factory party at Christmas!

What else do I need to know?

A good financial adviser, especially if your worm farm takes off.

The hidden threat

The worms of course might catch on to what you're up to and refuse to co-operate. Although if this happens, see next entry!

Wild bird

These do not make good pets. Which is really why they're called "wild", I suppose. Likewise injured birds can often recover faster if you don't touch them, but simply leave them where they are. Obviously if they're in your cat's mouth then this is probably not a healthy environment, but handling a wild bird can be enough to kill it. If you recover an injured bird from your cat (or dog, etc.), put it into a box with a lid on loosely, and leave it. It may get better on its own. If it doesn't – if it has a broken wing or something like that – it would be a good idea to take it to a vet. Sometimes baby birds fall out of the nest and need feeding. This is where your unco-operative worm farm comes in!

I'M GOING TO GET REALLY WILD IN A MOMENT!

X-Pet

What is it?

Well, the question should probably more accurately be "What *was* it?" It was your faithful, friendly pet. Well, "faithful" may be overstating things. Come to think of it, so might "friendly". But as with most things that pass, we only remember the good parts. It's sad, I know, but death is a fact of life. And pets are no exception. If your pet doesn't die of old age, but simply gets old and feeble, it is generally agreed to be much kinder to have it put down. Whether the pet would also agree if you consulted it is another matter.

What will it cost?

Most vets will destroy an animal for nothing, although some do charge. The rates vary enormously, depending on the animal. Some vets will come to your house and give your pet a lethal injection.[1] They may also take the animal away for you, although this is not always the case.

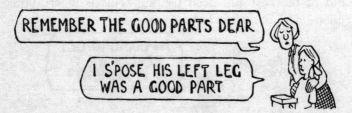

> REMEMBER THE GOOD PARTS DEAR

> I S'POSE HIS LEFT LEG WAS A GOOD PART

1: The vet will not appreciate you asking if he's got any spare for your little brother/sister, by the way.

Where will I keep it?

In the living room is not a good idea. You'll find that most animals begin to smell even more once they're dead. Some people like to bury their pets in the back garden. If you do this, make sure you bury it deep enough, particularly if you've got a dog.

What will it eat?

Nothing. It may help you to get over the grief to consider the saving you'll make on pet food.

What will it do?

Nothing. But then, in the case of some animals, this won't be much of a change really.

Why do I want it?

This is tricky to answer in this context. Why do you want it dead? Because it was ill. Why do you want it buried in the back garden? Because you were fond of it, and want to remember it. Or think you do.

When will it die?

It just has.

Will it earn its keep?

Erm . . . no. Although it might if it was stuffed.

What will I call it?

Dead, probably.

What else do I need to know?

Coping with death is never easy. If your pet dies, the most positive thing to do is to concentrate on the good times you had together, and remember your pet that way, rather than thinking about it when it was old or ill. Of course, if you can't remember any good times, then this can present a problem.

The hidden threat

Some pets can get at you even from beyond the grave. You find yourself wracked with guilt: was there anything I could have done to prolong its life? Did I feed it enough? Did I clean it out enough? Did I ever feed or clean it? Was I in any way responsible for its death? Should I really have been reversing Mum's car up the drive at 40 miles an hour when I'm only twelve and have never had driving lessons? Don't torture yourself! It's really not worth it. You can always make amends with the next pet – by not buying it!

Yak

Great coat – lousy pet.

Young

If you are breeding your pet(s), the chances are that it will have babies – if you're doing it properly, that is. Most animals are very protective of their newborn babies, and will kill them if you interfere with them. This strikes me as a very strange way of looking after them, but nevertheless it's a fact. So, if you don't want this to happen, the best thing to do is to leave the newborn babies alone until the mother is ready for you to see them, although you could be in for a very long wait!

Zoo

What is it?

There is no sight more pathetic than that of a small cluster of miserable moth-eaten creatures staring forlornly through the bars of a cage. And the animals don't look much happier. Zoos were largely established in the 19th century, to enable humans and exotic animals to stare at each other. Since then they have developed more into research centres, but they still get enormous criticism. It's not a debate I want to get into, though. Sorry!

What will it cost?

Zoos cost an enormous amount of money to run. Hardly any of them are cost effective, which is one reason why most of them are closing or closed. The strange thing is that the more a zoo attempts to recreate the animals' natural environment, the more it costs, and yet it doesn't cost a lion a penny to live in the wild. Possibly zoos should be set up exactly as per the wild, with animals breeding and eating each other. The only thing is that then, instead of signs to the visitors saying: "Do Not Feed the Animals", you'd need signs to the animals saying: "Do Not Eat the Punters".

Where will I keep it?

I'll take this to mean: *Where should a zoo be?*, shall I? Well, if we have zoos at all, they need to be somewhere where there is plenty of open land, so that animals have space. This of course is something we don't have a lot of in Britain, and even when we do somebody finds a way to build houses on it. The big game reserves in Africa and so on are a far better solution.

What will it eat?

Zoos don't eat anything – except money.

What will it do?

Arguably zoos provide a place for necessary research into ways of preventing animals becoming extinct. Although some simply provide a way to exploit a few poorly-kept specimens. But then, if zookeepers feel exploited and poorly kept, perhaps they should change their jobs.

Why do I want it?

I don't even know whether you do want zoos, but if you do then it's probably for all the reasons I've already outlined.

When will it die?

Zoos presumably will die out when people stop supporting them.

Will it earn its keep?

Probably not.

What will I call it?

Zoo would be a good name. Supermarket wouldn't.

What else do I need to know?

You can write to most zoos for information about their activities. Many of them run animal adoption schemes, whereby you pay a (smallish) sum of money, and this goes towards the upkeep of a particular animal. In theory at least. Obviously if nobody adopts a particular animal the zoo is still going to find the money to feed it from somewhere. But these schemes are a good way of ensuring an animal's survival.

The hidden threat

Animals in zoos are arguably at less risk of being poached.[1] The problem is that if too much energy goes into zoos, then maybe not enough attention will be given to improving controls over what happens to animals in the wild. We still have a long way to go to getting it right.

1: Or boiled or fried or baked.

A home of their own

While zoos – the good ones at any rate – obviously provide suitable homes for many wild beasts, and tailor-made cages can be obtained for most domestic pets, some animals do need special environments, if they are to survive in captivity. This next section deals with these environments, because –

YES!
HERE IT IS AT LAST!
THE BIT YOU'VE ALL BEEN WAITING FOR!
THE SECTION DEALING WITH THE MUCH TALKED ABOUT
*********TERRARIUM*********

What is a terrarium?

Well, basically a terrarium is a very swanky name for a fish tank. Except that it doesn't have water in it. Well, it might have a bit, but it wouldn't be full of water. If it was full of water it would be called an aquarium, and have fish in it as well, probably. If it was full of water and had animals in it, then it would be called a terrible accident. The common term for terrariums and aquariums is vivarium. So if the person in the pet shop says: "You look like you need a vivarium," that's what they're on about – they're not suggesting you have an operation. Although they might be. Actually, vivarium means an artificially created world, whether for fish or land creatures, OK? Well, I'm glad we've got that sorted out!

Playing God?

In creating a vivarium you are constructing a corner of the world specifically tailored to the needs of the

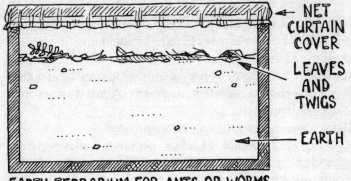

NET CURTAIN COVER

LEAVES AND TWIGS

EARTH

EARTH TERRARIUM FOR ANTS OR WORMS

WIRE MESH COVER

FRESH LEAVES

BRANCHES, GRASS, TWIGS ETC

GARDEN TERRARIUM FOR CATERPILLARS

SAND, ROCKS, HOLLOW LOG, POND ETC

OPTIONAL EXTRAS

TERRARIUM FOR SNAKES

particular pet you intend to keep. Make sure that it's big enough for the pet concerned. Incidentally, if you're thinking of buying a lion for a pet, don't bother with a terrarium because a) you probably wouldn't be around long enough to complete it, and b) you'd need a tank the size of Sidcup.[1]

Basic requirements for any vivarium are:

1) *Fish tank*: Made of glass or strong plastic. But whatever it is, it must be see-through, because there's no point in having the pet if you can't see it! So don't use a cardboard box, especially if you intend keeping fish!

2) *A lid*: You'll need to cover your vivarium to prevent your pet(s) escaping. Make sure you use something that allows air to get into the tank, though. Wire mesh is a good idea, clingfilm isn't.

Once you've got your tank and your lid, you need to think about what to put in it. The mini-world you create will depend entirely on its inhabitants. For instance, if you want to keep an assortment of garden creepy-crawlies, then try and create something that resembles a corner of your own garden – minus the empty Coke cans, bits of rotting barbecue food, fag-ends and dog's poo, obviously. Here's a few pointers:

ANTS: Fill your tank three-quarters full with earth, and spread garden debris (leaves, etc.) on top.

CRICKETS: Earth, then twigs, branches, grass, etc.

CATERPILLARS/SNAILS, ETC.: Earth, leaves, twigs, moss, etc.

SNAKES/LARGE SPIDERS/LIZARDS, ETC.: Sand, rocks, branches, a small rock pool, hollow log, etc.

1: For the information of foreigners, aliens and people who can't read maps, Sidcup is in southern England and is about the size of a large safari park. It has several supermarkets, full of people, so any lion living there would not go hungry.

WORMS: Plenty of earth, with garden debris on top.

NITS: Not really suitable for keeping in a terrarium, because you'd need a human head!

Also bear in mind that your terrarium might need watering, or extra heat. After all – the sun shines occasionally, and it rains all the time! Try to match the climate of the terrarium to that of the country of origin of the pet. If you're in any doubt, check with the shop where you bought the pet.

Twisting by the pool

Obviously some creatures require water, either to drink or to splash about in. You can create a simple pool by sinking a shallow jar lid into the earth or sand in the bottom of your terrarium and filling it with water. Make sure it's shallow, unless you want your pet to drown! You can of course be more creative and construct a pool out of tin foil, plastic moulding or even plaster of Paris. But don't get too complicated because you will have to change the water occasionally! Also bear in mind that if your pet likes to drink water, you will need to put this in a separate container. After all, you don't want to encourage it to drink its own bath water, do you?

Fishy business

Aquariums obviously require different setting up. Instructions on how to do this will normally come with the aquarium when you buy it. A word of warning: the instructions will probably start: "Remove packaging and throw away." The throwing away instruction refers to the packaging, not the aquarium!

A word of warning

Just because you've got your pet(s) in a terrarium, don't imagine that they never need cleaning out. They do, so these pets are no easy option. For example you'll need to change the water, dust the logs and twigs for "droppings" in some cases, and remove rotting food. If you don't do this regularly, you might find yourself having to remove the rotting corpse of your pet instead.

Creeping up on the creepy-crawlies

Having created a terrarium you'll need to find things to put in it. This is assuming that you didn't obtain the pet(s) first. Now, in the case of many pets, this is not a problem. You just go to a shop and buy them. And if you're setting up a garden terrarium, then a lot of creatures, such as caterpillars, are big enough simply to pick up. But in the case of an ant colony or a terrarium containing very small insects and bugs, you will need a bug-catcher.

Pooting your bugs

A bug-catcher, or pooter to give it its proper name, is really very simple to make. All you need are the following:

Jar with screw-top lid
Two bendy drinking straws (different colours)
A small piece of net curtain or muslin
A reel of sticky tape or sticking plaster.

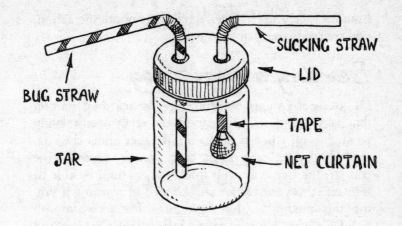

BUG STRAW

SUCKING STRAW

LID

TAPE

NET CURTAIN

JAR

What to do:

Make two round holes in the lid of the jar, the right size for the straws to fit tightly through. If the holes are a bit big, just wind tape around the straw until they fit tightly. If the holes are a lot too big, or square, just go "oops!" and start again! One of the straws needs to be pushed almost all the way to the bottom of the jar. The other one just goes in a few centimetres. The short straw is the "sucking" one, and will need a bit of muslin or net taped over the end inside the jar (*see illustration*) to prevent you swallowing your pet before you've had time to enjoy it!

It is a good idea to use two different coloured straws. This will prevent you sucking the wrong straw, always assuming you can remember which colour is which! Give your pooter a quick test-run. You could use a grain of rice as your bug. Place the grain on a flat surface[1] and try and suck it into the jar. If it works, great! If it doesn't, check that you've got the pooter the right way

1: The top of your little brother's head is only any good if he's completely bald!

round. Once you have perfected your pootering action, you are ready to catch your pet.[1]

Bearding a bigger bug

Of course if you are confronting – or *bearding* – a bug that is too big to poot, and you really don't fancy picking it up, you can slide a bit of paper under the bug, then plonk a jam jar over the top. Then, by inverting the jam jar, the bug will drop into it, and you'll be able to transfer it to your terrarium. A word of warning if you use this method – don't go away for a two-month holiday abroad between putting the jar over the bug and inverting the jar, otherwise all your efforts will be wasted, and all you'll have is a dead bug, and a funny smell.

1: I must stress that a pooter is only useful for very small creatures. Trying to suck up anything the size of a gerbil could give you a very nasty strain.

Keep On Petting

Well, I hope you've found this book useful. Naturally you would need a book the size of Norway to house information on every animal, but I have done my best to cover a pet cross-section.[1] All that remains for me to say is enjoy your pet, but don't forget that however well you treat it, it is still basically in captivity, and some animals adjust to this easier than others. So please, please bear this in mind and treat your pet with great care and a good deal of respect. I firmly believe that if you do this then your pet will reward you by . . . Well, by sitting in a corner and sulking, when it's not trying to bite your arm off, probably. But, still, what can you do? It is an animal after all, just like we are!

HAPPY PET-KEEPING!

1: In some instances an extremely cross section. Some animals just do not like being pets, or petted, or any of that nonsense!

Appendix: quick reference

Here's a quick guide to pets, their cost, where they live, what they eat, and star ratings based on how interesting they are, and their suitability as pets. I hope you find it useful. (NOTE: The greater the number of stars, the more interesting or suitable the pet is.)

PET	COST	HOME	FOOD	INTEREST	SUITABILITY
ANT	free	terrarium	bread/honey/meat	*	**
BUDGIE	£5–10	cage	seed	*	****
CAT	varies	house	meat	****	*****
CATERPILLAR	free	terrarium	leaves	*	*
CHICKEN	£3–10	pen/run	chickenfeed	**	**
CHIPMUNK	£25	large cage	fruit/nuts	***	**
DOG	varies	house	meat/biscuits	****	*****
FISH	varies	aquarium	fish food	***	****
GERBIL	£3.50	cage	seeds/fruit	***	***
GUINEA PIG	£5 +	cage	veg/cereals	**	***
HAMSTER	£5	cage	hamster food	*	**
MOUSE	50p	cage	oats/fruit	*	*
PARROT	£300 +	cage	seeds/fruit	–	–
PONY	£600 +	stable	oats/pony food	*****	*
RABBIT	£5–15	hutch	hay/cereals	***	****
RAT	£3.50	cage	oats/nuts	****	*****
SNAIL	free	terrarium	leaves	–	–
SNAKE	£15 +	terrarium	small rodents	**	–
SPIDER	£25 +	terrarium	crickets	*	–
TREE FROG	£30 +	terrarium	flies/crickets	**	–
WORM	free	terrarium	garden debris	***	****

You'll notice that some creatures have a (–) instead of a (*) in their column. This is because they didn't rate at all in that category – sorry!